Paternal Ancestry
Anne Brydges
Edward Brydges
John Brydges
Robert Brydges
Jemima Egerton
William Egerton LLD
Jane Gibbon
Anne Head
Hester Busby
Sir Frances Head
Margaret Smythbye
Elizabeth Langlois
Peter Langlois
Julie de la Mellonière
Phoebe Thompson
Anthony defroy Merchant
Deborah Young
Edward Gibbon
Martha Roberts
Hon Thos Egerton
Judith Mainwaring
Frances Head
Sarah Cul
Sir W. Smythbye
Sir James Smythby
Sir George Cul
Richard Head
Sir W. Mainwaring
Sir John Busby
Jane Bunce
John Roberts
Ferdinand Stanley
Alice Spencer
John Austen
Elizabeth Weller
Mary Howard
Weller
Young
Addee

Jane Austen's World

DEDICATION

To Peter Troy
who found out more about Jane Austen
than he ever thought he wanted to know

This edition published by
Adams Media Corporation
260 Center Street, Holbrook, MA 02343
by arrangement with Carlton Books Limited.

ISBN 1-55850-748-5

Printed and bound in Great Britain

A B C D E F G H I J

CIP information available upon request from the publisher.

Project Editor: Sarah Larter
Art Editor: Zoë Maggs
Designer: Vicky Harvey
Picture research: Maja Mihajlovic
Production: Sarah Schuman

Jane Austen's World

THE LIFE AND TIMES OF ENGLAND'S MOST POPULAR AUTHOR

Maggie Lane

Adams Media Corporation
Holbrook, Massachusetts

Contents

Introduction

IN THE PAST, JANE AUSTEN has always been regarded as an acquired taste, a connoisseur's choice for those who delight in the delicate play of irony and wit, and romance which is thoughtful rather than passionate. Recently, however, her novels have entered the best-seller lists, a sudden jump in popularity, which has been stimulated by the recent crop of film and television productions.

Why is it in the 1990s that Jane Austen should have gained such mass appeal, on both sides of the Atlantic, is an intriguing question. Perhaps it is because the novels are so free from scenes of sex and violence. Perhaps it is because their fictional world provides so total an escape from everyday life. Escapism of one kind or another may be the answer, but there are more positive reasons, for the world of Jane Austen is not simply a scene of Regency romance. Her heroines engage our attention. We are encouraged to share their problems, to understand their values and see them through the eyes of their creator – an ironic, amused and quizzical gaze that invites us to think about them as well as to feel for them as they tread their paths to marriage.

The books about Jane Austen are countless. To my knowledge however, *Jane Austen's World* is unique. It provides a series of vignettes of Jane Austen at various times in her life, of her family and friends, her interests and enthusiasms, her writing, from the earliest childhood pieces to the great novels. And beyond this immediate focus is the setting of the larger world, from the great issues of politics, war and slavery to the cultural realms of landscape gardening, the picturesque, spas, resorts and fashion. Jane Austen once wrote that "3 or 4 Families in a Country Village is the very thing to work on", yet the novels take in a larger scene, and the great value of Maggie Lane's approach is in its placing of Jane Austen clearly and firmly in an historical setting. We are able to see how the concerns of the Regency period, its society and culture are present in the novels themselves – for example, the issues of Empire and Slavery that enter *Mansfield Park* or the events of the Napoleonic war that run throughout *Persuasion*.

I am sure that *Jane Austen's World* will be welcomed by readers of all ages. Some will want to work through the book systematically from the earliest years of Jane Austen's life to the present day and "Jane Austen and Ourselves". Other readers will want look up a specific topic or area. However we use this book, its greatest service will be to turn us to the novels themselves with greater insight, understanding and affection.

BRIAN SOUTHAM
Chairman, The Jane Austen Society

Jane Austen's life

1764
The Reverend George Austen marries Miss Cassandra Leigh. First home Deane Parsonage, Hampshire.

1767
Austens move to Steventon Rectory.

1773
Birth of Cassandra Elizabeth, 9 January, the Austen's fifth child and first daughter.

1775
Birth of Jane, 16 December, seventh child and second daughter.

1782
Cassandra and Jane sent to boarding school run by Mrs Cawley in Oxford.

1783
Mrs Cawley moves her school to Southampton. The Austen girls catch typhoid fever and are brought home to Steventon, where Jane very nearly dies.

1785–1787
Cassandra and Jane attend the Abbey School at Reading.

1787
Her formal education finished, Jane begins to write and preserve the scraps collected into *Volume the First*.

1788
Family visit to Great-Uncle Francis Austen at Sevenoaks, in Kent.

1793
Last pieces in *Volume the Third*. Birth of nieces Anna and Fanny Austen (later Knight).

1795
Elinor and Marianne written.

1796
First preserved letters of Jane Austen date from this year.
JANUARY: flirts with Tom Lefroy.
SEPTEMBER: visits brother Edward and his family at Rowling in Kent.
OCTOBER: begins *First Impressions*.

1797
AUGUST: finishes *First Impressions*.
NOVEMBER: the Reverend George Austen offers the manuscript to the publisher Cadell, who declines to look at it.
Begins *Sense and Sensibility*. Visits Bath with Cassandra, staying with Uncle and Aunt Leigh Perrot.

1798
Begins *Susan*. Visits Edward and his family at their new home, Godmersham in Kent. Birth of nephew and future biographer, James Edward Austen (later Austen-Leigh).

1799
Finishes *Susan*.
MAY–JUNE: visits Bath with mother, Edward and family, staying in Queen Square.

1800
NOVEMBER: visits friend Martha Lloyd at Ibthorpe in Hampshire. On return home, learns of parents' decision to retire to Bath.

1801
FEBRUARY: visits Bigg family at Manydown.
MAY: leaves Steventon, stays with Leigh Perrots in Bath, family house-hunting.
MICHAELMAS: lease taken on 4 Sydney Place, Bath.
SEPTEMBER: holiday in Sidmouth.

1802
Holiday in Dawlish and Teignmouth.
NOVEMBER: Harris Bigg-Wither proposes.

1803
Susan sold to publisher Crosby.
NOVEMBER: Holiday in Lyme.

1804
Move to Green Park Buildings, Bath.
SEPTEMBER: Holiday in Lyme.

1805
JANUARY: death of Revd George Austen. *The Watsons* begun and abandoned.
Moves to Gay Street (spring) and again to Trim Street (autumn).
AUGUST: visits Godmersham.

1806
JULY: leaves Bath forever.
Tour through Gloucestershire, Warwickshire and Staffordshire.
Lodgings in Southampton.

1807
Austen women take house with brother Frank and wife in Castle Square, Southampton.
SEPTEMBER: visit Edward at Great House, Chawton.

1808
JUNE: visit to Godmersham.
OCTOBER: Edward offers Chawton cottage.

1809
APRIL: writes to Crosby asking about *Susan.* Austens leave Southampton, family visits until Chawton Cottage ready for occupation in July.

1810
Preparing *Sense and Sensibility* for publication.

1811
FEBRUARY: *Mansfield Park* begun.
APRIL: Visits brother Henry and his wife Eliza in London.
NOVEMBER: *Sense and Sensibility* published by Egerton.

1812
NOVEMBER: copyright of *Pride and Prejudice* sold to Egerton.

1813
JANUARY: *Pride and Prejudice* published.
MAY: Visits Henry and Eliza at Sloane Street.
JULY: finishes *Mansfield Park.*
SEPTEMBER: visits the widowed Henry at Henrietta Street.
SEPTEMBER–NOVEMBER: Godmersham.
NOVEMBER: Second editions of *Sense and Sensibility* and *Pride and Prejudice.*

1814
JANUARY: *Emma* begun.
MARCH: visit to Henrietta Street.
MAY: *Mansfield Park* published.
AUGUST–SEPTEMBER and again NOVEMBER–DECEMBER: visit to Henry at Hans Place.
Correspondence with Anna Austen about novel-writing.
NOVEMBER: Anna marries Ben Lefroy and ceases to write.

1815
AUGUST: *Persuasion* begun.
OCTOBER–DECEMBER: visits Henry at Hans Place, nurses him through serious illness, deals with new publisher (John Murray). Visits Carlton House library and corresponds with librarian James Stanier Clarke.
DECEMBER: *Emma* published.

1816
MARCH: Walter Scott publishes highly favourable notice of *Emma* in *Quarterly Review.*
AUGUST: finishes *Persuasion.*
Illness begins. Visits Cheltenham with Cassandra seeking cure.

1817
JANUARY: begins Sanditon.
MARCH: abandons *Sanditon* because of ill health.
MAY: moves to Winchester, with Cassandra, for treatment.
JULY: dies and is buried in Winchester Cathedral.
DECEMBER: *Persuasion* and *Northanger Abbey* posthumously published with Biographical Notice written by Henry.

CHAPTER ONE

Who was Jane Austen?

"WE HAVE NOW ANOTHER GIRL, a present plaything for her sister Cassy and a future companion. She is to be Jenny ... ". So the Reverend George Austen, Rector of Steventon and Deane in Hampshire, announced in a letter to his sister-in-law the birth of one of the world's greatest novelists. Jane – for she was never, at least after infancy, known as Jenny – was his seventh child, but welcomed into the family every bit as warmly as the earlier ones.

From both parents she inherited exceptional abilities. As she grew up, the family provided her with both the security and stimulation necessary to set her off on the path of writer. Her sister Cassandra was just the close companion their father had foreseen; her clever brothers were a source of fun, encouragement and intellectual stimulation. Her home and neighbourhood – a large country rectory in a well-ordered hierarchical society – were further vital sources of security, while a period spent in Bath, though unwelcome at the time, imparted maturity to her character and greater depth to her writing.

Given that all this conspired to provide the best possible conditions for nurturing her genius and bringing her vision to triumphant expression, those of us who marvel over the power of her novels to amuse and edify afresh generation after generation are still left with the question – who was she? What kind of woman did she appear to those who knew her? What were her attitudes, values and beliefs? How did she cope with her gifts as a writer – or rather, with the paradox, for the times, of being both a woman and a writer?

There have been many interpretations of Jane Austen in the two hundred years that separate her lifetime from our own. There is Jane Austen the untaught genius, creating her perfect miniature works of art almost unconsciously in the intervals between sewing and paying calls – the view of Henry James. There is the sharp, knowing spinster who writes from her head, not her heart, a view to which D.H.Lawrence and Charlotte Brontë both subscribed. There is the cosy "Aunt Jane" image, an approach her own family cultivated, of a woman whose life was spent in dutiful domesticity, unclouded by any kind of worry and modestly avoiding male topics like money and war. And there is the angry, subversive Jane Austen – or rather, Austen – the proto-feminist, diligently discovered by (mainly female) academics of our time in universities all over the world.

It is clear that these interpretations tell us almost as much about their authors as about the subject of their enquiry. She was a complex woman, the products of whose brain are so many-layered and inexhaustible that they have the power to speak meaningfully, but differently, to every age. We must all weigh the evidence for ourselves, reach our own conclusions, and allow for truth to be more elusive than myth. This is one of the most intelligent, self-aware women of all time that we are trying to pin down. We must be prepared for her to outwit some of our attempts.

But for those who love the novels, the attempt will always be worth making. By approaching her through her own letters and portraits, the evidence of the novels and other writings, and the recollections of people who knew her, it is possible to build a composite picture of Jane Austen as an individual, before setting her in the context of the family, friends and places who helped to make her what she was.

The Woman

SILHOUETTE, PROBABLY OF JANE AUSTEN, C. 1802.

AS JANE AUSTEN'S FAME spread and grew after her death, people who had known her were called on to record their impressions. More casual, passing references to her have also come down to us in letters written during her lifetime by family members and slight acquaintances. These sources supplement what we know or surmise of her from the primary evidence of her own writings. Taken all together, they reveal Jane Austen as she developed from a gifted child to a self-aware and complex woman.

Appearance

We know quite a lot about Jane Austen's appearance and how it struck others. All the descriptions left by those who knew her tally in certain particulars. She was tall and slim, with curly dark brown hair, large round hazel eyes and – what people tended to notice most – an exceptionally high colour in her cheeks. In her youth she seems to have been accounted a very pretty girl, her looks enhanced by a glow of health, animation of figure, and eyes that must often have been sparkling with fun.

Unfortunately these are not charms that always outlive carefree youth. In Jane Austen's case it seems they did not. The anxieties and frustration experienced in her late twenties seem to have robbed her early of her looks. The tall thin figure became a little unbending: "a poker" was the description attached to her by somebody who knew her slightly later in life. Her small mouth was apt to look pinched, and it is not difficult to imagine an expression in those piercing bright eyes that people might find intimidating. Her family continued to see "cheerfulness, sensibility and benevolence" in her expression, because she loved them and was relaxed in their company. To strangers she presented a typically spinsterish look. Both Jane and her sister wilfully encouraged this image by taking to the garb of middle age – most notably the wearing of caps indoors – much earlier than their nieces, for example, thought necessary. One wonders why the sisters chose to do this; presumably it was to fend off the indignity of seeming to remain in the marriage market beyond their time.

Character

Jane Austen was born with a sunny temperament, inherited from her father. With the exception of her eldest brother, who suffered from melancholy, all of the Austen children were of cheerful disposition, affectionate, intelligent and lively; but among them Jane was particularly playful and demonstrative of her feelings. Though she could be shy with strangers, at home her cleverness, openness and high spirits must have made her a delightful child. For the first twenty five years of her life she appears to have been as consistently happy as her own creation Emma Woodhouse. Adulthood brought depth and shade to her character. Her comic vision of life and literature did not leave her, but delight in the ridiculous became something more measured and controlled. Her playfulness was subdued; she learnt to take life seriously in these middle years. She remained capable of great tenderness of heart – toward her family, toward the creatures of her imagination – but her acute critical faculties were used now to confront not the absurdities of literature, but the the real and sometimes painful facts of existence.

In the final, fulfilled years of her life she managed to regain much of her old equilibrium and contentment, though the new sombreness of spirit was not far beneath. Her niece Anna Austen Lefroy remembered her in maturity as being less uniformly cheerful than her sister. Not a moody woman, she was nevertheless capable of different moods:

> *Her unusually quick sense of the ridiculous inclined her to play with the trifling commonplaces of everyday life, whether as regarded people or things; but she never played with its serious duties or responsibilities – when she was grave she was very grave.*

This is what we would expect of a woman who thought deeply about life.

Jane Austen and her heroines

Although all the heroines are highly individual and none is an attempt at self-portraiture, some do possess characteristics and attitudes that seem to derive from their author.

ELIZABETH BENNET: "It was her business to be satisfied – and certainly her temper to be happy." Witty, spirited Elizabeth Bennet has more of the youthful Jane Austen in her than any other heroine. "As delightful a creature as ever appeared in print," was her author's verdict.

EMMA WOODHOUSE: "A mind lively and at ease, can do with seeing nothing and will see nothing which does not answer." By giving a playful imagination to her faulty heroine Emma, Jane Austen explores something of her own novelist's cast of mind.

JANE AUSTEN'S NIECE ANNA LEFROY WHO CHERISHED VIVID RECOLLECTIONS OF HER AUNT.

Jane Austen called Emma "a heroine whom no-one but myself will much like" – though readers do.

ANNE ELLIOT: "Saved as we all are by some comfortable feeling of superiority from wishing for the possibility of exchange, she would not have given up her own more elegant and cultivated mind for all their enjoyments." This is not arrogance, it is proper self-esteem, in which Jane Austen's most mature heroine – though "almost too good for me," – surely resembles her creator.

ANNE ELLIOT, WHOSE "ELEGANCE OF MIND AND SWEETNESS OF CHARACTER" RESEMBLE JANE AUSTEN.

The Writer

FROM HER EARLIEST TEENAGE YEARS until a few months before her death, with the exception of one unhappy fallow period, Jane Austen was engaged in writing fiction. After her family, it was the most important thing in her life. Before she reached her twenty-second birthday she had a manuscript ready to submit to a publisher, and though it was many years before she actually saw her books in print, when at last they began to be published she relished not only the acclaim but the earnings they brought her.

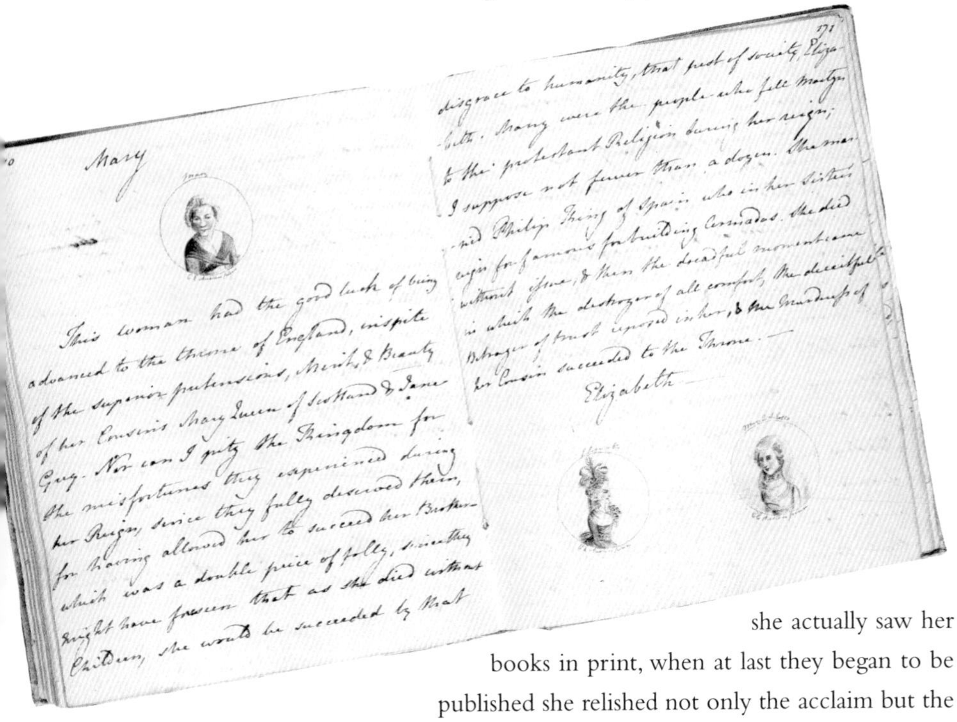
Mary

This woman had the good luck of being advanced to the throne of England, inspite of the superior pretensions, Merit, & Beauty of her Cousins Mary Queen of Scotland & Jane Grey. Nor can I pity the Kingdom for the misfortunes they experienced during her Reign, since they fully deserved them, for having allowed her to succeed her Brother — which was a double peice of folly, since they might have foreseen that as she died without Children, she would be succeeded by that

171

disgrace to humanity, that pest of society, Elizabeth. Many were the people who fell martyrs to the protestant Religion during her reign; I suppose not fewer than a dozen. She married Philip King of Spain who in her sister's reign was famous for building Armadas. She died without issue, & then the dreadful moment came in which the destroyer of all comfort, the deceitful Betrayer of trust reposed in her, & the Murderess of her Cousin succeeded to the Throne. —

Elizabeth

MANUSCRIPT OF "A HISTORY OF ENGLAND BY A PARTIAL, PREJUDICED AND IGNORANT HISTORIAN", WRITTEN WHEN JANE AUSTEN WAS JUST SIXTEEN YEARS OLD.

The Juvenilia

The young Jane Austen began writing to amuse her family, whose custom was to read aloud in the evening family circle. The Austens were "great Novel-readers and not ashamed of being so," subscribing to a private lending library for the purpose. The Sentimental novel and the Gothic novel, two of the most popular genres of the time, attracted many minor practitioners whose efforts were exaggerated, inconsistent and absurd. Jane took up her pen to parody and poke fun at these effusions. So bright was her wit and so lively her intelligence that the scraps she wrote for her family's amusement between the ages of twelve and sixteen still have the power to make us laugh out loud – despite the passage of two hundred years and the fact that the originals that inspired her have long since been forgotten.

Early attempts at publication

Reading the juvenilia, we can observe the process whereby the nonsensical fragments written in her youth gradually became more substantial and more deliberately grounded in reality, with believable characters making their mistakes and moral choices against a background of contemporary life. In her twentieth year (1795) she was working on a novel in the form of letters which she called *Elinor and Marianne*. Next she completed a straightforward narrative novel known as *First Impressions*. It was this manuscript that her father, on her behalf, offered to the publisher Cadell – who declined even to look at it. Undeterred, she immediately went back to her novel in letters, recast it as narrative, and renamed it *Sense and Sensibility*. The following year, inspired by a holiday in Bath, she wrote a new novel known as *Susan*. Between the ages of nineteen and twenty-four, when most young ladies would have been preoccupied with courtship and marriage, Jane Austen had written three major novels, one of them twice over. It was a quite extraordinary burst of creativity. She must have felt so close at this stage to realizing her ambition of becoming a published writer. In fact a dozen years were to elapse before she did so, years in which sometimes she must have despaired. In 1803 she sold the manuscript of *Susan* to the publisher Richard Crosby for the meagre sum of £10. He advertised the work as forthcoming, but never actually set it up in type. Waiting with hopes raised and gradually fading must have been more disappointing than downright rejection.

Another novel was begun but abandoned after a few chapters. The family had left Steventon Rectory for Bath, which unsettled Jane. In 1805 her father died and with him his income, throwing the widow and two daughters on to the charity of the Austen sons. Jane, her mother and sister moved from lodging to lodging, first in Bath and then in Southampton. These were Jane Austen's bleakest years, when her literary activity was minimal. She made various alterations to manuscripts in hand, but originated no substantial work. Then her fortunes changed.

The published novels

In 1809 the Austen women moved to the village of Chawton in Hampshire, where once again they enjoyed the benefits of a settled home in the country. Immediately, Jane Austen experienced a surge of renewed confidence in her destiny as an author. She decided to take the risk of publishing at her own expense, a perfectly respectable form of publishing then, and chose *Sense and Sensibility* with which to do so. The novel came out in 1811; her self-confidence was justified, as it made a reasonable profit. Her publisher, Thomas Egerton, offered to buy the copyright of her next work. This was *Pride and Prejudice*, a revised and shortened version of *First Impressions*, which appeared in 1813. At the same time she was working on the first of three freshly conceived novels. *Mansfield Park* came out in 1814 and *Emma* in 1815. *Persuasion* was published posthumously at the end of 1817, together with *Susan*, bought back from Crosby and renamed *Northanger Abbey*.

THE TABLE AT CHAWTON COTTAGE WHERE JANE AUSTEN IS THOUGHT TO HAVE WRITTEN.

There was thus a second intensive bout of creative energy, resulting in three "Chawton" novels to equal the achievement of the three "Steventon" novels. The last six or seven years of her life were intensely busy and happy, occupied with composition, making fair copies, proof-reading, dealing with publishers and enjoying the public reaction to her work, whether reviews or opinions of friends. When she became ill and died in 1817, having laid aside the beginning of a new work, she was at the height of her literary powers.

Jane Austen's earnings

Although she published anonymously, the "secret" of her authorship soon became known, and she wrote semi-humorously of intending to make all the money rather than all the mystery that she could from her work. "Tho' I like praise as well as anybody, I like what Edward calls Pewter too" and "I have now … written myself into £250 – which only makes me long for more" are two examples from her letters which show how important her earnings were to her. It has been calculated that she made about £630 during her lifetime; she did not spend any of this money but invested it against old age. In fact Cassandra Austen was to inherit most of this sum, and garner about a further £1,000 in royalties after Jane's death.

Cassandra's memorandum

SOME TIME AFTER HER SISTER'S DEATH, CASSANDRA AUSTEN WROTE DOWN THE DATE OF COMPOSITION OF THE NOVELS. HER NOTE READS:

First Impressions begun in Oct 1796
Finished in Augt 1797.
Published afterwards, with alterations and contractions under the Title of Pride & Prejudice.

Sense & Sensibility begun Nov. 1797
I am sure that something of the same story and characters had been written earlier and called Elinor & Marianne

Mansfield Park, begun sometime about Feby 1811 – Finished soon after June 1813

Emma – begun Jany 21st 1814, finished March 29th 1815

Persuasion begun Augt 8th 1815
finished Augt 6th 1816

Northanger Abbey was written about the years 98 & 99

C.E.A.

Beliefs and Values

JANE AUSTEN WAS A DIDACTIC NOVELIST – that is, one who created her imaginary worlds not only for the delight of creation, but to put forward certain moral values. Part of her purpose in writing was to be a good influence on her readers and therefore, in some small way, on her society. Without such a purpose, she would have thought the writing of fiction sheer self-indulgence, a childish pleasure to be given up on reaching a responsible age.

A practical Christianity

The moral that runs through all Jane Austen's novels is that we should control our own selfish impulses, be regardful of other people's feelings and make the best of whatever life happens to bring us. These were precepts taught to her in childhood and practised, as far as possible, by all the Austens as a religious duty. Jane Austen was brought up in the Church of England during one of its most serene periods, and she appears to have suffered no crisis of faith. Hers was a practical Christianity, a left-over from the eighteenth-century, focused more on living decently as a member of society than on the individual's relationship with God. Among her writings is one prayer, in which she seeks God's help in judging other people less harshly and herself more severely. In her novels, the characters who incur their author's disapproval are almost all careless of the comfort of the people among whom they happen to live. For Jane Austen, there was hardly an obligation stronger than the exercise of self-control in the interests of social and domestic harmony. Although there are very few references to religion in the novels, it does in fact underpin all the efforts of the worthy characters to know their duty and behave with decency.

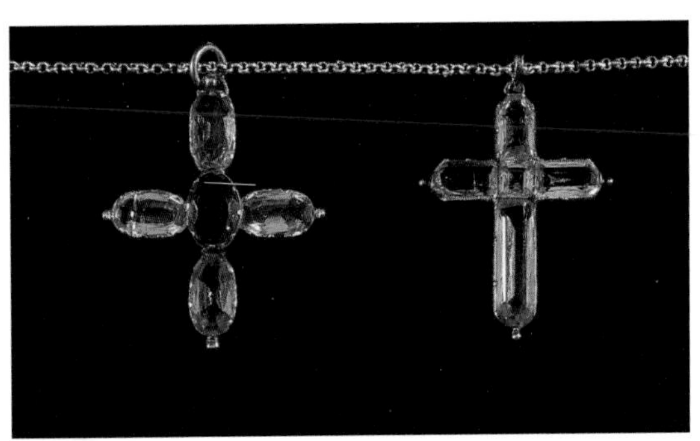

TOPAZ CROSSES GIVEN TO JANE AND CASSANDRA BY THEIR YOUNGEST BROTHER CHARLES.

Snobbery

Jane Austen has sometimes been accused of being a snob. This misconception probably arises because she deals only with a certain level of society. Servants and members of the labouring classes appear in her novels only as adjuncts to the protagonists, never as individualized characters. We simply have to accept that what interested Jane Austen was the kind of subtle moral dilemma that only people with leisure and education were likely to confront. The most shocking snob in the novels is Emma Woodhouse – particularly shocking because otherwise there is so much that is good and lovable about her. But Emma is at fault in her assessments of other people, and we are not expected to share her view. The correct attitude is that of Mr Knightley, whose respect and friendship for Robert Martin his tenant farmer, and William Larkin his farm bailiff, are among his many attractive qualities. By the end of the novel, Emma has at least partially acknowledged the error of her ways. The other snobs in the novels are incorrigible and Jane Austen has no time for them. They include the cold-hearted pair Lady Middleton and Fanny Dashwood; Fanny's mother Mrs Ferrars; Sir Walter Elliot and two of his three daughters; and Lady Catherine de Bourgh. Simply to name these characters is to realize how little Jane Austen sympathizes with snobbish views. Lady Catherine's attempt to exact from Elizabeth Bennet a promise not to accept Mr Darcy is based on

LADY CATHERINE DE BOURGH FROM "PRIDE AND PREJUDICE", WHOSE CHARACTER ILLUSTRATES MANY OF THE VALUES JANE AUSTEN DESPISED.

nothing but snobbery for Lady Catherine makes no allowance for Elizabeth's personal qualities. Every reader rejoices when Elizabeth fails to be cowed.

The accusation of snobbery is also sometimes made against Jane Austen in connection with the Portsmouth scenes in *Mansfield Park*. Fanny Price loses all her romantic illusions about her old home in the back streets of Portsmouth and before the end of the week is longing to return to the elegant style of living at Mansfield Park. Fanny deplores the slovenly ways of her parents and can find no love in her heart for them. Some readers find this as shocking as Emma's outrageous views. But the animus against the Price household is not snobbery on their author's part, as she proves by her praise of the younger generation of Prices. Their sterling qualities, as Sir Thomas Bertram himself reflects at the end of the novel, have been formed by "the advantages of early hardship and discipline, and the consciousness of being born to struggle and endure". There could hardly be a less snobbish assessment than that.

Money and materialism

Though Jane Austen valued the elegancies of life that money could buy, nothing was as important to her as human affection. Once, staying in a wealthy household, she contrasted the French wine drunk there with the home-made wine of her own home: "Luckily the pleasures of Friendship, of unreserved Conversation, of similarity of Taste & Opinions, will make good amends for Orange Wine".

Jane Austen's own strong wish of earning money was not avarice – she spent nothing of what she earned – but the desire not to be a burden on her brothers, who had families of their own. While only too aware of the dreadfully precarious position of women without money in her society, she consistently deplores marriage without love. At the same time, she is no advocate of marriage unless there is enough money to live on. In Jane Austen, both prudence and the impulses of the heart must be in balance.

The Letters

AS A MEMBER OF A LARGE letter-writing family, Jane Austen must have written many thousands of letters in her lifetime, only a small percentage of which are extant. Nevertheless, enough remain to give a reliable outline – with a few regrettable gaps – of the course of her life from the flirtatious girl of 1796 to the resigned invalid of 1817. Reading the letters we share her thoughts as she mixes in society, matures, enjoys her literary success and eventually prepares for death. They are full of her personal opinions, wittily expressed, and of insights into the everyday life of the time.

Letter-writing in Jane Austen's day

Letters were written on large pieces of paper, which would be folded into four and sealed with wax for posting, one quarter of one side being left blank to take the address. Envelopes had not been thought of; neither had stamps. The recipient paid for the letter on the basis of number of sheets (not weight) and distance. In 1812 the cost of a single sheet varied between four and seventeen old pence. Cross-country posts had been established in Jane Austen's childhood, encouraging the practice of letter-writing in the country homes of the middle classes. In London there were between four and eight deliveries per day; Marianne Dashwood sends, receives or enquires for letters before breakfast, in the evening and at all points between. Members of Parliament had the right to send letters free, a perk known as franking, which was often abused – even by the upright Sir Thomas Bertram. Fanny Price is astonished when Edmund assures her that her first letter from Mansfield to her brother will be franked by her uncle.

In sending a letter without benefit of a frank, one had to believe that the recipient would judge it worth the cost. If there was a great deal to say a second set of lines would be written at right angles across the first, making the "checkerwork" that Miss Bates refers to in *Emma*. Jane Austen and Cassandra often partly crossed their letters to one another. "A long letter" in their parlance meant one into which a great number of lines had been squeezed; Jane mentions admiringly 42 lines to the side in one of Cassandra's.

A LETTER IN JANE AUSTEN'S HANDWRITING ADDRESSED TO HER BROTHER FRANK ON BOARD THE BATTLESHIP HMS ELEPHANT.

The letters to Cassandra

Of the surviving letters, most are addressed to Cassandra. Whenever the sisters were apart – one of them paying a family visit which might last several weeks – they wrote to each other every day. As soon as one letter was posted, another would be begun, and added to over a period of three or four days. In the meantime the reply to the last would be received, so each letter was likely to begin with the writer's latest news and then respond to the incoming letter. This system ensured that the sisters kept in constant communion with each other, something that appeared to be essential to their well-being.

These sisterly letters are full of the minutiae of life that each knew would interest the other; as Jane once began a letter, "Which of all my important nothings shall I tell you first?" Because of the concentration on domestic detail and news of family and friends, when they were first published in 1932 the letters caused some disappointment in the literary world. They were thought trivial and gossipy – unworthy of a great novelist. With the rise of feminism, that attitude has been discredited. Women's lives and concerns are now granted to be as important to women as men's are to men, and to speak just as profoundly of the human condition. Not only that, but in their turn of phrase, sparkling wit and acute observation of the people around her, Jane Austen's letters are now recognized to be cut from the same fine-textured cloth as the novels: a minor work of art in themselves.

"Even if Jane Austen had no other claim to be remembered, her letters would be memorable. Read with attention, they yield a picture of the life of the upper middle class of that time which is surely without a rival."

(R.W. CHAPMAN)

None of Cassandra's side of the correspondence survives. She kept all Jane's letters to her but some time before her own death went through them destroying any that contained material she considered controversial. These probably included references to bodily functions as well as critical remarks about family members and any evidence of unhappiness or repining on Jane's part. What remains therefore is a slightly sanitized selection, which has reinforced the impression of Jane Austen as the most untroubled of our great authors. However, because Jane Austen was incapable of writing a bland sentence, the letters that escaped Cassandra's censorship cannot fail to give a picture of a truly original mind in all its varieties of playfulness, thoughtfulness and feeling.

Other correspondence

Letters exist from the last few years of Jane Austen's life that were addressed to recipients other than Cassandra. Many of her nephews and nieces kept her letters to them. Those to her niece Anna are especially interesting as they contain almost all her surviving reflections on the art of the novelist.

Among the admirers of Jane Austen's novels was the Prince Regent, who invited her, through his librarian James Stanier Clarke, to dedicate her next novel to him. This she dutifully if reluctantly did, the novel being *Emma*. Clarke appears to have been rather smitten with the author when he showed her, by royal request, round the library at Carlton House. He inveigled her into a correspondence, pompous on his side, tongue-in-cheek on hers, in which she fends off his absurd suggestions for the kind of novels she should write.

POSTMAN COLLECTING MAIL C. 1827. THE POSTBOX WAS NOT INVENTED UNTIL THE MIDDLE OF THE CENTURY BY THE NOVELIST ANTHONY TROLLOPE.

The Portraits

There is only one authentic portrait of Jane Austen, the watercolour sketch by her sister Cassandra now in London's National Portrait Gallery. Although all the Austen brothers had their portraits professionally painted at some time in their lives, the sisters were neither rich nor important enough to have themselves recorded for posterity the same way. Even when Jane Austen was a published novelist, becoming known to the reading public and frequently visiting London, the question of having her portrait professionally painted does not appear to have arisen. Or if it did, she was too modest to agree to sit. There is no serious mention of the subject in the letters: merely her joke, in November 1813 when, after reporting that people are starting to get curious about "what I am like & so forth" she adds "I do not despair of having my picture in the Exhibition at last – all white & red, with my Head on one Side".

THE ONLY CONFIRMED LIKENESS OF JANE AUSTEN, PAINTED BY HER SISTER CASSANDRA.

Cassandra's sketch

Cassandra appears to have been a competent amateur artist. While Jane wrote, Cassandra painted and drew. In their youth, she illustrated her sister's hilarious *The History of England, by a Partial Prejudiced and Ignorant Historian* (see p.14) with watercolour medallion portraits of thirteen monarchs mentioned by Jane, in which, no doubt to carry on the joke, they all appear as Georgian gentlemen and ladies.

Several other pictures by her survive, figure studies and landscapes. Presumably Jane Austen must have sat to her sister, if only casually, innumerable times in the course of their forty-one years together. The fact that this particular picture survives surely indicates that Cassandra and Jane were reasonably satisfied with it.

After Jane's death, those who had loved her would surely not have wanted to keep a picture that they felt was a travesty. At some point it seems to have been given to Charles Austen, whose descendants eventually sold it in 1948. The portrait was described then as "a pencil sketch ... the face and hair in watercolours" and estimated to date from about 1810.

Cassandra's competence as an artist and the very fact of this portrait's preservation are arguments in favour of its being a true representation of Jane Austen's features and expression. So is the undoubted family resemblance to the professionally painted portraits of the brothers and of Jane Austen's father. The Austen's facial features were all variations on the theme of a small mouth and large dark eyes. On the other hand, Jane's niece Anna Lefroy, writing in the 1860s, thought the sketch was "hideously unlike".

The Victorian versions

When Jane Austen's nephew James Edward Austen-Leigh came to write his *Memoir* of his aunt in his own old age, he knew that the public for the book would be curious about her appearance. He therefore sought a portrait for the frontispiece. His sister Anna argued against using Cassandra's sketch as it stood, for as we have seen she did not think it did her aunt justice. Nor did it conform in the least to Victorian ideals of submissive womanhood. This was bad enough. But there was another reason for the family to be dissatisfied with Cassandra's sketch. That an apparently unfinished amateur drawing should be the only likeness of their illustrious aunt that the family could produce reflected badly on them in such snobbish times. It implied that earlier generations of Austens had been uncouth and impoverished. Therefore Austen-Leigh commissioned a tidied-up reworking of the sketch as well as an engraving for reproduction in the *Memoir*. In both these versions the facial expression is made milder, the features better proportioned and the background more highly finished. These images are often used even today in preference to Cassandra's sketch. But there is nothing authentic about them; they are Victorian versions of Jane Austen with the original sharpness smoothed away.

The full length view

The only other picture known to be of Jane Austen unfortunately does not show her face – but it is a charming figure piece, and has often been reproduced in modern times. A watercolour, it is signed and dated "C.E.A. 1804". Anna Lefroy refers to it as "a sketch which Aunt Cassandra made of her in one of their expeditions – sitting down out of doors on a hot day, with her bonnet strings untied". This picture is still in possession of a descendant of the family through the Francis Austen line. (see p.10)

THE 1869 ENGRAVING, WHICH SOFTENS AND ELABORATES CASSANDRA'S EARLIER PORTRAIT FOR A VICTORIAN AUDIENCE.

The silhouette

In 1944 a silhouette of a young woman was found pasted into a second edition of *Mansfield Park* with the hand written inscription: "L'aimable Jane". What other Jane, it was argued, would be inserted into a novel by Jane Austen? This is slender evidence, but it is very possible that the sisters had their silhouettes taken while they were living in Bath, as did both their parents. It was a much cheaper process than portrait painting, and was fashionable in the Regency period. The National Portrait Gallery thought well enough of its claim to authenticity to acquire the silhouette, albeit cautiously cataloguing it as "identity uncertain". In the last few decades various pictures have been put forward by their hopeful owners purporting to be of Jane Austen. All seem to be a case of wishful thinking. The wish to have another view of her is a very natural one, but until much better evidence is produced than we have yet seen, we must rest content with the famous sketch by Cassandra.

Family Background

MINIATURE OF THE REVEREND GEORGE AUSTEN, JANE'S FATHER, WHO WAS ADMIRED IN HIS OLD AGE FOR HIS ABUNDANT SNOW-WHITE HAIR AND BRIGHT EYES.

JANE'S PARENTS, the Reverend George Austen and his wife Cassandra, née Leigh, were well-matched in character and intellect, but they came from rather different social backgrounds. The Austen family belonged to the entrepreneurial and professional classes; the Leighs were of the landed gentry with aristocratic connections. What George and Cassandra did have in common was that they came from the poorer branches of their respective families; neither of them had any private fortune.

George Austen's family

Generations of Austens had made a comfortable living in the Weald of Kent as farmers and clothiers – that is, men who organized the manufacture of woollen broadcloth on the cottage industry system: early capitalists, in fact. They owned two substantial houses, Broadford and Grovehurst, near Horsmonden, where church memorials testify to the family's local importance. The family prosperity was not shared equally, however. Jane Austen's great-grandmother Elizabeth Austen was left a penniless widow with many children to raise, only her eldest son being provided for. Though she had not been brought up to work for her living, she swallowed her pride and took the post of housekeeper at Sevenoaks School so that her younger sons might have the benefit of a free education. Thereafter each was apprenticed to a profession. Francis was the most successful, becoming a solicitor in Sevenoaks and purchasing a fine old Queen Anne property in the town, known as the Red House. Another son, William, became a doctor, which was not a very high status profession in the eighteenth century, but died young, leaving two small children, Philadelphia and George. Kind uncle Francis paid for his orphan nephew's education at Tonbridge School and St Johns's College Oxford. Clever and studious, George Austen was destined for the church. After his ordination he combined the post of Usher (second master) at his old school with the curacy of a nearby parish. At the age of twenty eight, he become proctor of St John's, where he was known as "the handsome proctor" on account of his open, smiling face and bright dark eyes. He seems to have combined a love of scholarship with a serene temperament and a cheerful readiness to take on work. It is no wonder that Cassandra Leigh fell in love with him, despite the difference in class.

Cassandra Leigh's family

The Leigh history goes back to the time of the first Elizabeth, when Thomas Leigh, a lord mayor of London, received his knighthood. One of his grandsons was created Lord Leigh of Stoneleigh Abbey in Warwickshire by Charles I, while another line of the family owned property at Adlestrop in Gloucestershire. The Leighs of Adlestrop were connected by marriage to the Duke of Chandos, whose second wife, Cassandra Willoughby, brought her unusual Christian name into the family and gave her maiden name to one of Jane Austen's most charming characters. The Duke of Chandos's sister, Mary Brydges, having married Theophilus Leigh, bore him twelve children before dying in childbirth at the age of thirty seven. One of her sons was Thomas, so precociously clever that he was known as "Chick Leigh" at Oxford, which he attended at a very young age. Another son, Theophilus, was to be Master of Balliol College for more than fifty years. "Are you not delighted with his gaiety of manners and youthful vivacity, now that he is eighty-six years of age?" Mrs Thrale wrote of him to Dr Johnson. These two brilliant men were Cassandra's father and uncle respectively.

There was therefore a heritage of intelligence and good humour on both sides of Jane Austen's family. Cassandra Leigh delighted in word-play and all her life maintained the habit of writing occasional verse for her own and others' amusement. She expressed herself more forthrightly and epigramatically than her mild husband, and prided herself on her common sense: what she herself called her "sprack wit". Her granddaughter remembered her as:

> *A little slight woman with fine well-cut features, large grey eyes and good eyebrows, but without any brightness of complexion. She was amusingly particular about people's noses, having a very aristocratic one herself, which she had the pleasure of transmitting to her children ... She was a quick-witted woman with plenty of sparkle and spirit in her talk who could write an excellent letter in either prose or verse with no pretence to poetry but simply common sense in rhyme.*

The marriage of George and Cassandra

Cassandra Leigh grew up at her father's rectory of Harpsden in Oxfordshire, but in 1760 he retired with his wife and two daughters to Bath, then in its heyday as a fashionable resort. Cassandra was probably visiting some of her many relations in Oxford when she was introduced to George Austen by Thomas Powys, a mutual friend. When George Austen and Cassandra Leigh married in St Swithin's church at Walcot in Bath, in April 1764, it was Powys – who was later to become Dean of Canterbury – who conducted the ceremony. George Austen was enabled to contemplate marriage and family responsibilities because of the continuing generosity of his own relations. A distant wealthy cousin, Thomas Knight, who owned estates at Godmersham in Kent, and at Steventon and Chawton in Hampshire, presented George Austen with the living (that is, the rectory and stipend) of Steventon in 1761. Not to be outdone, Uncle Francis Austen purchased the adjoining living of Deane for his deserving nephew. George and Cassandra Austen began their married life at Deane, while Steventon Rectory was refurbished to their liking, after which they let Deane Rectory for additional income.

Cassandra Austen took on the cares of running a large household on a moderate income, while bearing eight children. George Austen not only managed two parishes conscientiously but took in pupils and farmed land, which he rented from Thomas Knight. It was a hardworking and highly successful partnership, providing an exemplary foundation for family life.

SILHOUETTE OF CASSANDRA AUSTEN, JANE'S MOTHER, WHO WAS PROUD OF HER ARISTOCRATIC NOSE AND HER COMMON SENSE.

Home at Steventon

JANE AUSTEN WAS BORN at Steventon Rectory, which remained her home for the first twenty-five years of her life. It provided her with all the security and stimulation required to foster her talent. Here she grew up in the midst of a large and lively family; here she came to consciousness within a stable wider community, where everybody, including the younger Miss Austen, knew exactly their place in the world: what was owed to them and by them. More a hamlet than a village, Steventon is tranquil and remote today: even more so then, when roads were poor and communications non-existent. Yet the Austens lived sociable lives, visiting all the neighbouring gentry. Because George Austen was known to be related to the landholder, and because the manor house of Steventon was let to tenants, the Austens were accorded a higher social status than some clergy families. They were even included in invitations to Hurstbourne Park, home of the Earl of Portsmouth, and Hackwood Park, home of Lord Bolton, when those noblemen gave balls.

At the other end of the social scale, the Austens paid charitable visits to the poor parishioners, knowing the inhabitants of every cottage in Steventon and Deane. The villagers turned to Mrs Austen for baby clothes and for advice on whether they should grow the strange new crop, potatoes; and to Mr Austen to settle such matters as "whether Paris was in France or France in Paris". It all contributed to that sense of social and spiritual rootedness in one spot that Jane Austen so much valued and which was to do so much in shaping her art.

The rectory

Steventon Rectory was demolished in the 1820s, considered unfit to house the new generation of clergy. Certainly it was an unpretentious house. The front door opened directly into one of the two reception rooms; the windows were old-fashioned casements, not sashes; there were no cornices

SKETCH BY ANNA AUSTEN LEFROY OF STEVENTON RECTORY, JANE AUSTEN'S CHILDHOOD HOME WHERE THE FIRST THREE OF HER NOVELS WERE WRITTEN.

between wall and ceiling; the ceilings themselves were low, with exposed beams whitewashed over; and the cellar was liable to flood. Whatever its deficiencies in nineteenth-century eyes, however, to the family who occupied it during the last quarter of the eighteenth century it was a beloved and perfectly adequate home with many comforts. George Austen had a study at the back of the house, where he accumulated his library of 500 volumes, wrote sermons and gave lessons. On either side of the front door were the dining-parlour, and the sitting-room where Mrs Austen continued to apply herself to her pile of mending even when visitors called. There were seven bedrooms and three attics, enough to stow away two or three boarding pupils besides the Austens and their servants.

As the brothers grew up and left home, space was released for the two girls of the family, who shared a bedroom all their lives, to appropriate an adjoining room as their private sitting-room. We know that it had two windows, a fireplace and a dark brown patterned carpet. Here they kept their books, piano, sewing, drawing materials and writing desk; here Jane Austen's earliest experiments in fiction were made and some of the greatest novels in the language brought into being. No matter that it had "scanty furniture and cheaply papered walls". From an early age Jane Austen enjoyed that vital precondition for a creative life, according to Virginia Woolf, "a room of one's own".

The garden and farm

The Austens were great gardeners and were making constant improvements to the rectory garden right up until the moment they left. At the front of the house they made a gravel drive for the carriage, sweeping between trees and turf. This was their concession to fashion. The garden at the back of the house, sheltered by thatched mud walls as was the custom in that part of the country, mingled beauty and utility, flowers and vegetables. Indeed, with the exception of citrus fruit, which had to be bought, all the fruit, herbs and vegetables consumed by this large household were home-grown. They also kept poultry, and bees for honey and mead. The production, processing and storage of food occupied a great deal of space. Though the front of the house presented a symmetrical facade, the back of the house was irregular and rambling, with many outbuildings such as brewhouse, bakehouse and dairy, all the province of Mrs Austen. Traditionally, land known as glebe was attached to most parsonage houses for the cultivation of food. At Steventon the glebe amounted to three acres, but Mr Austen also rented the 200-acre Cheesedown Farm from Thomas Knight. Though he employed a bailiff, John Bond, Mr Austen took an active role in the management of the farm, which produced all the family's meat as well as wheat, barley, oats and hops. Surplus produce was sold to bring in extra income. Jane Austen therefore knew what it was to live close to the land and to be governed by the cycle of the seasons. There is nothing spectacular about the scenery in this part of north Hampshire, but Jane Austen, who was a great walker, loved it for its familiarity and because it was good, working, productive land. She was proud to be "a Hampshire-born Austen".

CHURCH OF ST NICHOLAS, STEVENTON WHERE MR AUSTEN WAS RECTOR. JANE AUSTEN ONCE MADE PLAYFUL ENTRIES IN THE MARRIAGE REGISTER.

The six brothers

CAPTAIN FRANCIS AUSTEN, THE FIFTH OF JANE'S SIX BROTHERS.

JAMES (1765–1819) was, after Jane herself, the most literary of the Austens. At Oxford University he founded and largely wrote a satirical magazine; all his life he wrote poetry – not the light verse in which all the family indulged from time to time, but rather turgid, sub-Wordsworthian reflections on nature. A fine classical scholar like his father, he was always intended for the church. It was also tacitly assumed that he was the heir to his wealthy childless uncle, James Leigh Perrot, after whom he had been named. On his marriage he became his father's curate at Deane, and eventually his successor at Steventon. His first wife died when their daughter was only two; by his second wife he had two more children. Jane Austen called him "good and clever", though she did not think his temper his finest point.

James was the most introspective of the Austens, and the only one to possess a streak of melancholy in his nature. There is reason to think of him as a disappointed man. His literary ambitions came to nothing, and it was difficult for him, the clever eldest son, to see his younger sister – a woman! – succeed where he had failed. He never came into his Leigh Perrot inheritance, though his son eventually did so; James had to observe a younger brother, Edward, succeed to wealth and position while he remained an obscure country clergyman.

GEORGE (1766–1838) was mentally retarded, subject to fits, maybe deaf. With a ruthlessness difficult for us to comprehend today, he was excluded from family life. He was boarded out for the whole of his long life with labouring people in a village a few miles from Steventon, who looked after him for the sake of a few pounds a year.

EDWARD (1767–1852) had the good fortune to be adopted in his youth by George Austen's patron Thomas Knight and his wife, who were childless. Edward inherited all their property, Godmersham in Kent, where he resided, and the Hampshire estates, Steventon and Chawton. Edward's wife died in 1808 bringing their eleventh child into the world. In 1812 Edward and his children changed their surname to Knight. Though separated geographically and socially from the rest of the family, Edward remained close to them in every other way. Long visits to Godmersham were paid by the Austens of Hampshire, giving Jane extensive experience of country house life. After his father's death Edward made a generous allowance to his mother and sisters. Combining the Austen spirit of fun with an equable temperament and a head for business, Edward was well fitted for his role of country landowner, and was an affectionate and indulgent father, brother and son. All who knew him seemed to love him. "Good, amiable and sweet-natured" his mother called him; "especially delightful to all young people" a nephew said.

HENRY (1771–1850) was as clever as James but totally opposite in temperament: self-confident, eager and optimistic almost to excess. At one point he and James were both in love with the same woman, their widowed cousin Eliza, who was four years older than James and ten years older than Henry. It was Henry for whom she gave up "dear liberty". He must have had charm. Jane Austen certainly delighted in his company. He led the most chequered life of any of the Austens. Intended by his parents for the church, under Eliza's influence he rejected that career in favour of a commission in the army, where he made contacts that were useful to him later in establishing a London bank. Jane Austen derived her knowledge of London society chiefly through her visits to Henry's London homes. He was very helpful to her in dealing with publishers. A few years after Eliza's death (they had no children) Henry's bank failed, through no fault of his own, and in middle age he found himself setting out on a third career. He was ordained, and having missed out on all the best family livings, passed the rest of his life as a very poor curate, evincing extraordinary adaptablity and cheerfulness in the face of these reverses.

FRANK (1774–1865) and CHARLES (1779–1852) are often grouped together, being the two sailor brothers. Finding professions for sons at the tail end of a family was not easy in Georgian times, especially when the family had limited influence. It was hard for men to get on in their careers purely on merit. However, that is what both Frank and Charles succeeded in doing. Each joined the navy as a midshipman at the age of fourteen, and each rose through his own efforts to the rank of Admiral. Frank was even knighted, ending his very long life as Sir Francis Austen.

Frank was mild-mannered, courteous, diligent and practical. Charles had a greater share of the sunny optimism which descended from Mr Austen to several of his children. In his youth Charles was away for seven years without seeing his family, stationed in the West Indies and eventually bringing back a wife and child. Frank only just missed the Battle of Trafalgar, to his great disappointment.

Sympathetic to their deprivations and dangers, avid for their promotion, Jane Austen followed the naval careers of these brothers with keen interest. Through the experiences of Charles and Frank she was kept especially aware of the Napoleonic Wars and the wider world. Her knowledge of and respect for the navy appear in both *Mansfield Park* and *Persuasion*.

EDWARD, JANE'S THIRD BROTHER WHO CHANGED HIS SURNAME TO KNIGHT WHEN HE WAS ADOPTED BY RICH RELATIONS. THIS PAINTING WAS MADE WHEN HE WAS ON THE GRAND TOUR.

Some female relations

Cassandra

Jane Austen's sister, Cassandra Elizabeth Austen, was undoubtedly the most important person in her life. Born in January 1773, Cassandra was almost three years older than Jane, and was a calmer, more reserved personality. The relationship began with Jane very naturally looking up to her elder sister as knowing more and and having better judgement than herself, and an element of hero-worship seems to have remained all their lives. "If Cassandra were going to have her head cut off, Jane would insist on sharing her fate," Mrs Austen is reputed to have said when young Jane begged to be allowed to accompany her sister to school.

SILHOUETTE OF JANE'S SISTER CASSANDRA. "THEIR SISTERLY AFFECTION COULD SCARCELY BE EXCEEDED," A NEPHEW REMEMBERED.

Cassandra became engaged to a clergyman who had been one of her father's pupils, Tom Fowle. It was a long engagement. While Tom waited for a family living in Shropshire that was half-promised, he went as army chaplain on a military expedition to the West Indies in an effort to amass some savings. After some months without hearing from him, word made its way back to England that he had succumbed to yellow fever. The dignity and fortitude with which Cassandra bore the loss of her hopes impressed her young sister, whose heroines Elinor Dashwood and Anne Elliot demonstrate that a calm exterior does not imply lack of strong feelings.

If Jane admired Cassandra for her self-control, Cassandra delighted in Jane's gaiety and spirit. What the two sisters meant to each other is best expressed in Cassandra's own words, written to a niece immediately after Jane's death:

> *I have lost a treasure, such a Sister, such a friend as never can have been surpassed - she was the sun of my life, the gilder of every pleasure, the soother of every sorrow, I had not a thought concealed from her, & it is as if I had lost part of myself.*

If Jane had been the survivor, no doubt she would have said the same. Cassandra survived Jane by twenty eight years, continuing to live first with her very old mother and eventually alone.

Eliza

Fourteen years older than Jane Austen, Eliza was a first cousin who became a sister-in-law. Worldly and sophisticated, fluent in the French language, she basked in the admiration of the child Jane, and was very fond of her in her turn. Eliza had a colourful background. She was the daughter of George Austen's sister Philadelphia, who, while her brother was educated at his uncle's expense, had been shipped out to India, where a surplus of white men meant that any available white woman would soon be offered marriage. Within six months of her arrival, she found herself married to Saul Hancock, a man twenty years her senior. After eight years this loveless marriage produced one daughter – though it is highly likely that Eliza's father was in fact Warren Hastings, Governor of India, with whom Philadelphia Hancock had an affair. Certainly Hastings was godfather to Eliza, and left her money in his will.

Philadelphia and Eliza left India and spent some time in pre-revolutionary France. Eliza married the Compte de Feuillide and had one son by him, whom she named Hastings. Not long afterward the Compte was guillotined, a fate that helped to give Jane Austen a lifelong distrust of France.

Undaunted, the widow, with her mother and son, took up residence in England, where she conducted numerous flirtations, including simultaneous ones with her two Austen cousins, James – then a young widower – and Henry. These cousinly flirtations were carried on during the amateur theatricals that were then a feature of life at Steventon Rectory. Perhaps Eliza rejected James because he was a clergyman; certainly she persuaded Henry against becoming one. In all these manoeuvres she was being observed, though she did not know it, by a budding novelist. Eliza surely was the inspiration behind the charming though unprincipled Mary Crawford in *Mansfield Park*.

Anna and Fanny

These two nieces, both born in 1793, were just seventeen years younger than Jane Austen, and their affairs of the heart must have contributed something to the novels. Anna was the daughter of James by his first wife. When her mother died, Anna was sent to Steventon Rectory to be looked after by her two young aunts, and heard them reading aloud from early versions of *Pride and Prejudice* and *Sense and Sensibility*. A lot of what we know about Jane Austen comes from Anna's recollections. She retained a very affectionate memory of her aunt.

When James remarried Anna was called home, though she never got on with her stepmother. In her teenage years she was rather wild, cutting her hair short, entering into one ill-starred engagement and then breaking it off, then marrying Ben Lefroy, a man thought unsuitable by her relations. Meanwhile she had ambitions to be a novelist, making her particularly interesting to her aunt, whose letters to her on the subject of writing fiction are essential reading to the student of Jane Austen.

Fanny was the eldest daughter of Edward, and so eventually took the name of Knight. "Almost another sister" Jane once said of Fanny Knight. As a motherless, marriageable young woman she asked her aunt's advice on her various suitors, and the long, considered replies she received, and kept all her life, contain Jane Austen's thoughts on the subject of love and marriage.

WATERCOLOUR SKETCH BY CASSANDRA OF FANNY KNIGHT, ONE OF THE TWO NIECES TO WHOM JANE WAS EXCEPTIONALLY CLOSE.

Love and Friendship

JANE AUSTEN WAS A NORMAL young woman who enjoyed the attentions of the opposite sex in her youth, who expected to marry but remained philosophical when she did not. Unlike some of the more desperate marriage-seekers in her novels, she acted upon her belief that "anything is preferable to marrying without affection".

TOM LEFROY, WITH WHOM JANE ENJOYED A YOUTHFUL FLIRTATION.

She had two great compensations for not marrying or having children: her writing and her close relationship with Cassandra. It is doubtful whether as a wife and mother she would have been able to devote as much time as she wished to writing. Observing the toll exacted by continual childbearing on the women around her, she often expressed her distaste for such a fate. Yet marriage to a worthy man remained for Jane Austen woman's natural goal, the one to which all her heroines aspire.

A youthful flirtation

Just after her twentieth birthday, Jane enjoyed a brief flirtation with the visiting nephew of her friend Mrs Anne Lefroy, wife of the vicar of the neighbouring parish of Ashe. This highly cultivated lady had made a favourite of the young Jane. When Tom Lefroy came over from Ireland to stay with his English relations, it was natural that the two young people should often be in company together at the dances and dinners of local society.

Cassandra was away visiting her fiancé's family at the time, otherwise we would probably know nothing of the episode. "You scold me so much in the nice long letter which I have this moment received from you," Jane wrote to her on 9 January 1796, "that I am almost afraid to tell you how my Irish friend and I behaved. Imagine everything the most profligate and shocking in the way of dancing and sitting down together ... He is a very gentlemanlike, good-looking, pleasant young man, I assure you. But as to our having ever met, except at the last three balls, I cannot say much; for he is so excessively laughed at about me at Ashe, that he is ashamed of coming to Steventon, and ran away when we called on Mrs Lefroy a few days ago."

Tom departed a week later and Jane Austen never saw him again. Since in the same letter she remarks on the handsome eyes of another young man, it is clear that she was simply going through the youthful phase of testing her feelings for all the potential partners of her acquaintance. Tom Lefroy lived to be Lord Chief Justice of Ireland, and when asked in his old age about Jane Austen, he said that what he had felt for her had been "a boy's love".

The unnamed lover

Long after Jane Austen's death, Cassandra told one of her nieces that during their travels in the West Country, the Austens had met a young man who seemed even in her eyes to be worthy of Jane, and who was evidently attracted to her. They parted with agreement to meet again further on in their travels; instead, news of the man's death reached them. We know no more details. We can only guess that if it had felt like real love to Jane, then the disappointment would have been severe but she would have struggled to overcome it. In the fullness of time, she may have come to feel glad she had experienced that most precious of all human emotions, romantic love for another person, even though it had been the cause of sorrow at the time.

A rejected proposal

The love affair at the seaside probably happened in the summer of 1802. The following October, Jane Austen received her only known proposal of marriage. She was nearly twenty-seven; her suitor, remarkably, was just twenty-one. His name was Harris Bigg-Wither and he was the younger brother of Jane's close friends, Elizabeth, Catherine and Alethea Bigg. In the old Steventon days, on the nights of the Basingstoke assemblies, the Austen sisters had often stayed with the Biggs at their fine house, Manydown Park, nearby. Now living in Bath, Jane and Cassandra were paying a longer visit to their old friends.

One Saturday evening Harris proposed – with what degree of surprise to Jane Austen, we do not know – and was accepted. It would have been a good establishment for her, for Harris was heir to Manydown, and there were many circumstances in his favour. But she did not love him. She spent the night lying awake considering what she had done and first thing the next morning went to him and withdrew her acceptance. Feeling wretched in every way she and Cassandra insisted on sending for James to come over from Steventon to collect them immediately, even though it was Sunday. That alone shows the perturbation of her feelings. She had hurt the young man, disappointed his sisters, ill repaid hospitality and been guilty of vacillation. But she knew she had done the right thing. In due course calm returned, a settled lifestyle was achieved, thoughts of love and marriage seemed put behind her, and her novels came to take the place of the children she never had.

It is good to know that her friendship with the Bigg sisters remained unbroken to the end of her life. The three Lloyd sisters were also long-standing friends, Martha Lloyd, the only one remaining unmarried, eventually making a home with the Austens. Another good female friend was Anne Sharp, whom Jane met when she was governess at Godmersham, and with whom Jane continued to correspond.

MANYDOWN PARK IN HAMPSHIRE, HOME OF HARRIS BIGG-WITHER WHO ASKED JANE TO MARRY HIM.

Family Visits

JANE AUSTEN'S FAMILY connections on both sides were very extensive and scattered over southern and Midland England. The difficulties of travel did not prevent the Austens from enthusiastically visiting their relations, but having arrived at a destination after a journey taking two or three days, they were in no hurry to leave again. In the novels and in the life, family visits normally lasted several weeks, giving ample time to observe and become absorbed into a different lifestyle.

Kent

Jane Austen paid her first visit to Kent when she was twelve. With her parents and sister she stayed with great-uncle Francis in the Red House on the outskirts of Sevenoaks. Old Francis Austen must have been a formidable relation to encounter: her father's benefactor, then in his eighties, a man who had amassed great wealth not only through his work in the law but through marrying in succession two wealthy widows. His house and his garden, his clothes, his wig and his manners were all in the dignified style of fifty years or more back. Jane Austen was to return to Kent many times, but to East rather than West Kent, to the countryside around Canterbury and to houses brimming with the "elegance and ease and luxury" of contemporary, fashionable, country-house life. "Kent is the only place for happiness," she once half-jokingly remarked, "everyone is rich there".

In 1796 she stayed with her brother Edward and his wife Elizabeth in their first married home, a pleasant medium-sized house called Rowling, part of the Goodnestone estate belonging to Elizabeth's parents. Many sociable evenings were spent with Elizabeth's large family at Goodnestone, sometimes ending in an impromptu dance and a walk back across the park after supper.

A year later Edward inherited the mansion and estate of Godmersham from Thomas Knight. Over the next twenty years Jane and Cassandra often visited him there, usually separately. Jane Austen saw from the inside what it was like to live in a large, hospitable house, with multitudes of servants and rooms for every purpose. Her favourite of these was the library, where once she mentioned having "five tables, eight and twenty chairs and two fires all to myself". She wrote that somebody was always coming or going at Godmersham; as well as social calls, Edward had all the business involved in the management of a large estate, and his role as justice of the peace, to deal with. Her Godmersham experiences were both an education and a holiday.

STONELEIGH ABBEY IN WARWICKSHIRE, HOME OF MRS AUSTEN'S RELATIONS VISITED BY JANE AUSTEN IN 1806.

London

For somebody for whom it was important to experience and understand all facets of her society, Jane Austen was singularly fortunate in her brothers. As a London banker, Henry was able to offer her a place to stay in the capital and a chance to savour its diversions and mores whenever she wished. Henry did not, of course, move in the top circles in London – those were the preserve of the aristocracy with their houses taken for the season – but among the professional classes. Henry and Eliza held many parties, including a grand musical soirée which Jane Austen attended while a visitor to their house.

This was in Sloane Street, Knightsbridge, then an isolated development separated by marshland from the centre of town. It was here that Jane Austen corrected the proofs of *Sense and Sensibility*, the only novel, incidentally, with a London setting for a large part of the action. After Eliza's death Henry lived for a while over his bank in Henrietta Street, Covent Garden, convenient for the shops, theatres and exhibitions that Jane Austen visited from this address. Finally he moved back out to Knightsbridge, to Hans Place, where Jane Austen stayed with him in October 1814, when she was seeing *Emma* through the press. During this visit Henry had a severe illness which Jane helped nurse him through, while conducting her own dealings with her publisher; she also visited the Prince Regent's library at Carlton House.

A Northern tour

Only once did Jane Austen travel very far north of a line running from London to Bath. This was in 1806, when on leaving Bath and before settling in Southampton, Mrs Austen and her daughters made a protracted tour of their Leigh connections. They went first to Adlestrop, in Gloucestershire, where cousins of Mrs Austen occupied both the rectory and the mansion house. This was the village where Jane Austen's maternal grandfather, and all his forbears, had grown up.

By chance, during the visit Thomas Leigh, Rector of Adlestrop, found he had inherited Stoneleigh Abbey in Warwickshire from another branch of the family. He set out to visit his new property, taking the Austen women with him.

JANE AUSTEN'S GREAT-UNCLE FRANCIS, BORN IN QUEEN ANNE'S REIGN AND A YOUTH IN GEORGE THE FIRST'S.

Stoneleigh Abbey was extraordinarily grand – by far the largest house Jane Austen is known to have stayed in. A huge baroque slab, fifteen bays wide, had been added to the remains of the old abbey. With its interior chapel, Stoneleigh probably furnished hints for Sotherton Court in *Mansfield Park*, if not for Northanger Abbey itself. The tour terminated in several weeks spent at Hamstall Ridware in Stafforshire, where a nephew of Mrs Austen held a Leigh family living. Warwick Castle and the ruined Kenilworth Castle were visited *en route*. But, despite the fact some important scenes in *Pride and Prejudice* are set in Derbyshire, there is absolutely no evidence that Jane Austen ever set foot in that county.

Bath and the West Country

IN HER EARLY TWENTIES, Jane Austen paid two visits of several weeks duration to Bath, staying once with her uncle and aunt Leigh Perrot in the Paragon, and once in lodgings with Edward and his wife in Queen Square. Her experiences furnished materials for *Northanger Abbey*, in which the youthful heroine, Catherine Morland, observes life in a fashionable watering-place, deriving much innocent pleasure from its novelties and gaining necessary knowledge in the ways of the world. Catherine leaves the city at the end of her visit with no regrets. For Jane Austen too, Bath was all very well for a holiday. To live there permanently was another matter altogether.

When, in the autumn of 1800, she heard that her parents had decided to leave Steventon Rectory and retire to Bath, she is said to have fainted from shock. To live in a city represented a complete uprooting and reversal of the way of life she had always known – but at twenty-five and twenty-eight years old, the Austen sisters had no choice but to accompany their parents wherever they chose to live. Jane's feelings were to be mirrored in *Persuasion*'s Anne Elliot, who is also transplanted to Bath against her will.

More happily for Jane Austen, her parents' plans for their retirement included escaping the heat of the city in late summer and autumn by taking long holidays by the sea. And although the Bath years did turn out much as she feared, unsettled and unproductive, they were not all unhappy. Bath was a city that existed for pleasure. Though she might deplore some of its more snobbish and frivolous aspects, it would have needed somebody much more narrow-minded and sour-tempered than Jane Austen not to derive pleasure from it.

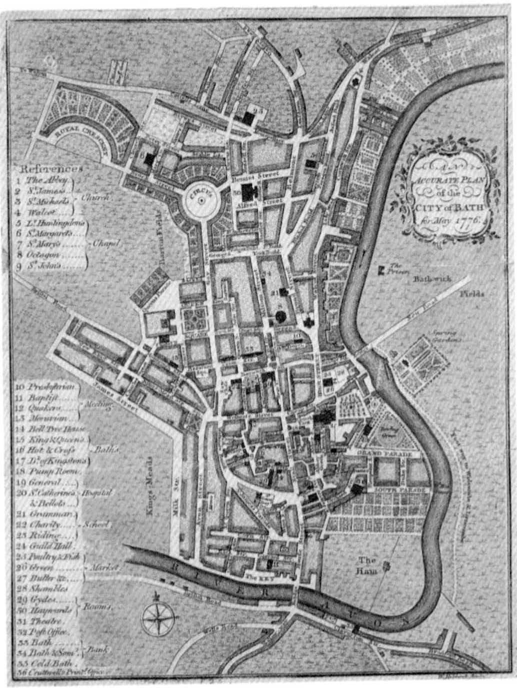

MAP OF BATH IN THE 1770S AT THE HEIGHT OF ITS FASHION.

Bath

The summer of 1801 was spent by the Austens house hunting in Bath. After rejecting many reasonably priced houses because they were damp or cramped, they settled in a new and fashionable part of town that they had at first thought too expensive for them, taking a three-year lease on 4 Sydney Place. The house was only nine years old, and the land behind remained undeveloped until after the Austens' time, so the rear of the property overlooked fields, while the front faced the public pleasure grounds of Sydney Gardens. The situation was a pleasant one, with a level approach to the centre of the city down the broad and handsome pavements of Great Pulteney Street.

It seems likely that Mr Austen's habitual optimism led them to take a house rather more expensive than they could really afford. At the end of the three years the lease was given up, and they moved to a terrace formerly rejected as too low-lying and damp, Green Park Buildings. At Steventon they had not only paid no house-rent, but almost all their food had been home-produced. Now everything had to be paid for in the shops and markets of Bath. And this out of a much-reduced income, for James had to be given part of the Steventon stipend to act as curate there. Had the Austens miscalculated? Certainly Jane's insecurity about money dates from the move to Bath. Perhaps suddenly feeling wiser than her parents, this was when she finally grew up.

Within a few months of moving to Green Park Buildings, Mr Austen died. The financial situation of his widow and daughters was now dire. Mrs Austen had a few investments bringing in £120 per year; Cassandra had inherited Tom Fowle's savings of £1,000, which yielded £50 per year; Jane had nothing. It was only because the brothers rallied round with offers of help that the Austen women were enabled still to keep a home going for themselves. Even so, in the next eighteen months they moved twice more in Bath. Unable to afford a whole house or the servants to maintain it – in Sydney Place they had employed two maids and a man – now they were reduced to a few rooms. This was Jane Austen's lowest ebb.

The West Country

In the summer of 1801 the Austens spent several weeks in Sidmouth, south Devon. The following year they visited Dawlish and Teignmouth, in the same county. In 1803 they went to Lyme in Dorset, returning there in 1804. All these resorts were in their infancy. They were connected to the major cross-country routes by very poor roads, often hazardous. Only recently had these little fishing communities been discovered by visitors in quest of the health-giving properties of sea-bathing and fresh air. The Austens were quite adventurous in taking up this new fashion for travelling to the sea in their old age. We know from one of Jane Austen's letters that it took them two days to travel from Bath to Dawlish, a distance of a hundred miles.

THE PUMP ROOM, BATH IN 1805 WHEN JANE AUSTEN WAS RESIDENT IN THE CITY.

Jane Austen loved the sea. She dwelt on its charms in all her later books. In *Mansfield Park* Fanny Price's spirits rise when she walks on the ramparts at Portsmouth and watches the sea dancing and sparkling in the sun. *Persuasion* is partially set in Lyme, described lovingly and, for Jane Austen, at length:

> *... the remarkable situation of the town, the principal street almost hurrying into the water, the walk to the Cobb, skirting around the pleasant little bay, which in the season is animated with bathing machines and company, the Cobb itself, its old wonders and new improvements, with the very beautiful line of cliffs stretching down to the east of the town*

In *Emma* the rival merits of Cromer and Southend are debated, and Emma herself finally gets to see the sea on her honeymoon. And the beginning of a new novel that she was forced to abandon in her final illness is all about a seaside resort, *Sanditon*.

Return to Hampshire

"IT IS TWO YEARS TOMORROW since we left Bath for Clifton, with what happy feelings of escape!" Jane Austen reminded her sister on 30 June 1808. Her next home was in Southampton, where the three Austen women, their friend Martha Lloyd, and Frank and his new wife Mary, took a house together. It made sense to share household expenses, and the others would be company for Mary, who was soon pregnant, when her husband was at sea. This arrangement lasted nearly three years and seems to have been a happy and harmonious one. The house they occupied for most of this period had a beautiful old-fashioned walled garden where once again they could grow fruit and vegetables. And it was pleasant to live by the sea.

CHAWTON GREAT HOUSE AND CHURCH IN 1809, THE YEAR THE AUSTENS SETTLED IN THE VILLAGE.

But late in 1808 an even more enticing prospect offered. Among Edward's property on his Chawton estate was a substantial cottage, formerly an inn, which had been occupied by Edward's bailiff. This man had recently died, and Edward offered the cottage to his mother, rent-free. Frank and Mary had already moved to the Isle of Wight. Edward's generosity extended to making certain alterations in the house to suit the more genteel tastes of a party of ladies. For example, the sitting room window, which was only a few yards from the public road, was stopped up and turned into a bookcase, and a new window of Gothic design was made to face over the garden. Meanwhile, Jane Austen's glee was expressed in doggerel, part of a rhyming letter to Frank congratulating him on the birth of a second child:

Our Chawton home, how much we find
Already in it to our mind
And how convinced, that when complete
It will all other houses beat
That ever have been made or mended
With rooms concise and rooms distended . . .

Even before they moved in, in July 1909, Jane Austen seems to have known that her writing would flourish here. She wrote to Crosby enquiring about the fate of her manuscript *Susan*. He offered to sell it back, an offer she was to take up only when Henry, transacting the business for her, was able to tell the discomfited publisher that the manuscript he had parted with so lightly was by the author of the successful *Pride and Prejudice*. Once they had settled in, she immediately began preparing *Sense and Sensibility* for publication. It was as if she knew her destiny had arrived.

Chawton

The village, about a mile from the little town of Alton, is a quiet one, though livelier in the Austens' day, when the roads to Winchester and to Gosport divided just outside their cottage. The space between the fork was occupied by the village pond, long since drained. Though the sitting-room window had been made to look over the garden, the dining-room, on the other side of the front door, could face nowhere but the road. This room was a

SOUTHAMPTON HIGH STREET, 1806. THE AUSTENS LIVED IN THIS CITY BETWEEN 1806 AND 1809.

favourite with Mrs Austen, who enjoyed watching the horse-drawn vehicles go by.

In this room too, Jane Austen's share of the household duties was to make breakfast, boiling the kettle for tea and making toast at the fire. Tea, sugar and china were kept in the alcove cupboard. That meal over, she was free to take up her writing, while Cassandra oversaw the rest of the housekeeping. Mrs Austen had long before resigned this responsibility to her elder daughter, but she was by no means idle herself. Sewing and gardening were her habitual occupations.

There were the usual kitchens and offices at the back of the property, and outbuildings round a little courtyard, where the washing, brewing and baking went on, and where the donkey-carriage they acquired was housed. The garden ran round the side and rear, with a good-sized lawn, plenty of trees and shrubs for privacy and shelter, a kitchen garden and flower-beds. Though the house had six bedrooms besides the attics, Jane and Cassandra continued to share a room. Their stock of nephews and nieces was constantly growing, and family visitors were numerous. Apart from the family and immediate neighbours, the Austens kept little company. Their taste and their means coincided. They made no pretensions to anything but a modest lifestyle, and they were content with a quiet, domestic life. Conditions were ideal for Jane Austen to conceive and perfect her great novels. The pity is that she had so little time left: just eight years of life at Chawton. But these eight years could hardly have been more productive and fulfilled.

Winchester

In May 1817 Jane and Cassandra moved to temporary lodgings in Winchester, to be under the care of an eminent physician there. Jane's health had been failing for about a year, of what we now suspect to be Addison's disease, a disorder of the kidneys. These days the condition can be kept under control by drugs, but nothing known at the time could prevent Jane dying on 18 July. Except for the debilitation of illness, she was at the very height of her mental and creative powers. She was buried in Winchester Cathedral, where a slab in the south aisle commemorates her personal qualities without mentioning the novels.

CHAPTER TWO

Daily Life in Jane Austen's England

LEISURE AND LITERACY, from being the preserve of the few, became much more widely diffused in the eighteenth century. The newly prosperous middling classes found themselves with hours and days to fill, largely as they pleased. Their inventiveness rose to the challenge, and social and domestic life acquired a variety of pursuits and pastimes, each governed by its own etiquette and conventions.

The sexes largely pursued their own occupations and pleasures in the morning, coming together in greater formality in the evening when, having eaten, they were expected to entertain one another with music, cards and conversation. Nobody could call their evening their own. Reading to oneself or writing letters were strictly occupations for the morning. After dinner, almost everyone had familial if not social obligations to fulfil, even if it is only Emma playing backgammon to while away the time for her father.

To this end, young women were expected to be accomplished in the various arts which could make a contribution to social life, especially music. Their education, unlike that of boys, was directed toward making them good value in the evening circle. In a sense this was their "work" in life until they were married. Most of the heroines accept this gracefully enough, Marianne Dashwood being the exception.

Even within the classes of which Jane Austen wrote, the amount of work required of individuals varied enormously. As far as the men were concerned, this is obvious enough. Only the most fortunate inherited estates which brought in an income sufficient to live on without working. The remainder had to have their professions, be it clergyman, soldier, sailor or lawyer. Among women there was a similar, if less visible, divide. Those like Lady Bertram who married men of large income could entrust the management of the household to a housekeeper. But many women of Jane Austen's class had to be their own housekeepers, supervising the servants and the day-to-day running of the house themselves. Nevertheless, with numerous servants and a host of material comforts unknown to previous generations, the people of Jane Austen's world were able to bring the art of living very close to perfection. This is one of the reasons why the novels are so popular, because they allow us to share lives which seem ordered, tranquil and elegant compared with our own. Of course we must not paint too rosy a picture. It is true that they lacked our resources against boredom, poverty, illness and pain. But at its best, the tenor of daily life combined the satisfaction of a useful role in society with the enjoyment of a host of pleasurable occupations.

Meals and manners

Breakfast

The breakfast of Jane Austen's day was eaten late, between nine and ten, often after some shopping, walking or letter-writing had been accomplished. Even something as simple as breakfast reflected the spirit of the age. Consisting of toast and tea, eaten and drunk from fine china, Regency breakfast was as different from the hunks of bread, cheese and ale of former times, taken from wooden platters and pewter mugs, as from the hot dishes of kedgeree, devilled kidneys, bacon and eggs and so forth under which Victorian sideboards groaned. Toast, which was made by the family themselves on toasting forks at the fire, was thought to have been invented by the English to enable the butter to spread more easily in their cold rooms. On the same fire the kettle would be boiled for the tea or, less usually, coffee. These drinks were still a novelty in English life, tea having been introduced from China, and coffee from Ethiopia, in the middle of the preceding century. Precious commodities, they were kept under lock and key, the responsibility not of the servants, but of the mistress. Their expense meant that hot drinks were not consumed throughout the day, as we are used to, but made their appearance only at breakfast and again in the evening. In grand houses a greater variety of fare was provided, but still not what we think of as the traditional English breakfast. Mrs Austen, staying at Stoneleigh Abbey, admiringly lists "Chocolate Coffee and Tea, Plumb Cake, Pound Cake, Hot Rolls, Cold Rolls, Bread and Butter, and dry toast for me".

TEA WAS TAKEN NOT IN THE AFTERNOON BUT MID-EVENING AND WAS A COSTLY AND HIGH-PRESTIGE DRINK.

The midday meal

Jane Austen uses the word "luncheon" once and "nuncheon" once, but both refer to midday meals taken at an inn. Refreshment taken by the family in their own homes in the middle of the day was a casual, stopgap affair that had not yet acquired the dignity of a name. Nor were social invitations ever issued for this meal, though if visitors were present, food would be offered – as Elizabeth Bennet experiences at Pemberley, where there is cold meat, cake and hothouse fruit; and Edmund Bertram at Mansfield Parsonage, where Dr Grant himself carries round the sandwich tray. This nameless midday snack of cold food and drink had arisen to fill the gap caused by the increasing lateness of the dinner hour.

Dinner

For centuries the English had eaten their dinner in the middle of the day, when it could be cooked and consumed in natural light. But in the eighteenth century, as leisure and prosperity increased, there was a gradual but constant shift in the dinner hour, with the most fashionable people always dining later than their social inferiors. That is, the dinner hour for all classes grew later as the century progressed; but at any one moment in time, the social status of a family could be gauged by when they dined. The Austens provide a striking example of the shift taking place within individual households. In 1798, writing from Steventon to Godmersham, Jane remarked, "We dine now at half after Three, and have done dinner I suppose before you begin ... I am afraid you will despise us." But by 1808 she could write, "We never dine now till five".

Dinner was the event of the day. The meal was as elaborate as the resources of the family would allow – that is, as the skill and number of their servants could produce. Multiple dishes of fish, meat and game would be placed on the table, together with a few side dishes of vegetables and two or three puddings. This was known as a "course", and everybody helped their neighbours to what they wanted. In grander households, the remains would be cleared away and a second similar "course" of savoury and sweet dishes would follow, with the emphasis this time less on great joints of meat and more on "made" dishes. Next the cloth would be removed and an assortment of nuts, sweetmeats, etc. would be placed on the table with wine; this was known as "dessert", and at this point the servants would withdraw. Finally the hostess would rise, at which signal all the other women followed her to the drawing room, leaving the men a further hour or so of drinking and uninhibited conversation in the dining room.

Tea

When Jane Austen mentions characters taking tea together, she is not referring to our "afternoon tea", which did not exist then, but to the serving of the beverage about an hour after the end of dinner, when the men would eventually rejoin the ladies in the drawing room. Sometimes invitations were issued just for this "tea" (sometimes coffee was also served), especially to social inferiors. Thus Harriet Smith, Jane Fairfax and Miss Bates are invited to the Coles "to drink tea", while Emma, Mr Knightley and the Westons arrive earlier to dine. Nobody seems to have taken offence at what seems a very offensive custom!

A TYPICAL COURSE AT DINNER WOULD INCLUDE A WIDE VARIETY OF DISHES AS SEEN IN THIS CONTEMPORARY MENU PLAN.

Supper

As dinner became later, supper dwindled to a negligible snack, usually something on a tray. The exception was on the evening of a ball. Then, late hours, great expenditure of energy and the prospect of a cold drive home called for real sustenance, which always included soup, and to drink negus – a mixture of boiling water, wine, lemon, spices and calves-foot jelly.

Housekeeping

Housekeeping occupied a great deal of female time and energy, especially in those households not rich enough to employ a housekeeper. None of the characters in Jane Austen's novels would have done their own cooking or housework, but many of them did have to give constant direction and guidance to the servants. This was the case with Mrs Austen, who ran a large household for forty years. Steventon Rectory was home to more than a dozen people, and virtually all the food they consumed was baked, brewed, churned, preserved and cooked on the premises. It was an enormous task. There is no doubt that Mrs Austen initiated her daughters into the domestic arts. Since they were highly unlikely to marry men rich enough to afford a housekeeper, they had to know how to manage a house themselves, perhaps on a limited income. Even women who did not marry might be called on to keep house for a widowed or bachelor brother or aged parents. In fact this is what happened to Cassandra, who in her middle twenties took over the role of housekeeper from her mother. Had Cassandra married or died, the role would have fallen to Jane.

As a general rule, Georgian women had far less done for them by servants than their Victorian counterparts. The Victorians would have thought such a life as Mrs Austen's a life of drudgery; we know that her own descendants thought so. At every level of society except the very highest, it was the unquestioned duty of every woman to be able to run a house efficiently.

THE VILLAGE BUTCHER. THERE IS A BUTCHER'S SHOP IN DELAFORD, MANSFIELD AND HIGHBURY, ALL PLACES ASSOCIATED WITH EMOTIONAL AND PHYSICAL NOURISHMENT.

Good and bad housekeepers

Though Jane Austen rarely follows her female characters into their kitchens, she gives enough hints for us to know how they measure up to this duty. For her, a good housekeeper is one who keeps within her budget, who creates a comfortable, well-ordered home for her family, and who is generous and hospitable to guests without being showy. Two contrasting housekeepers are the sisters Mrs Price and Mrs Norris of *Mansfield Park*. Mrs Price is incompetent and slovenly, with no control over her two servants; she is always behind-hand and her food is disgusting. Mrs Norris's fault is meanness. She economizes for its own sake, not out of necessity. It is an unpleasant characteristic, especially as she is always criticizing other people's wastefulness; but as Fanny Price concludes after suffering under her mother's roof, "Mrs Norris would have been a more respectable mother of nine children, on a small income".

A housekeeper who exceeds her income in her efforts to impress her neighbours is Mrs Bennet. Having married above her station, she suffers from social insecurity, which she attempts to allay with her boasts. She brags that unlike the family of Sir William Lucas, *her* daughters have nothing to do in the kitchen, but she is doing them no favours; how will Lydia, for example, ever manage a house on a small income? When Darcy and Bingley come to dinner, Mrs Bennet boasts that her soup was fifty times as good as Lady Lucas's, and that nobody had ever seen so fat a haunch of venison. Her most amusing boast, perhaps, is that the Bennets dine with four-and-twenty families.

To take pleasure in housekeeping is a virtue in Jane Austen. Her approval is bestowed on minor characters like Mrs Grant and Charlotte Collins, each of whom compensates for a less than happy marriage by deriving enjoyment from "her home and her housekeeping, her parish and her poultry, and all their dependant concerns". Women's lot might have been a very circumscribed one, but it could be made to yield its satisfactions for all that.

Housekeeping in town and country

One of the reasons why Jane Austen disliked living in a town the size of Bath was that food was expensive, sometimes adulterated, and – inevitably with slow transportation and lack of refrigeration – often less than fresh. Town milk was a case in point. To supply the population of Bath, cows were kept in the city itself, in cramped, unhygienic conditions, without access to fresh grass. The resulting milk was thin and poor, and was then often diluted with water before being hawked around the streets in open pails into which any dust or debris might be blown. In summer it must have been virtually undrinkable – perhaps one of the reasons why the Austens escaped to the sea every year. In *Mansfield Park*, as the warm spring weather advances during Fanny's sojourn in Portsmouth, she sickeningly observes "the milk a mixture of motes floating in thin blue". On the other hand, the shops and markets of Bath stocked a much wider variety of produce than was available in the country. As Mrs Allen observes in *Northanger Abbey*, "Bath is a charming place, sir; there are so many good shops here … One can step out of doors and get a thing in five minutes".

A THOMAS ROWLANDSON MARKET SCENE. THE AUSTENS BOUGHT FOOD AT THE MARKET IN BATH.

Living in the fashionable city of Bath, Jane Austen observed growth of retailing and availability of luxury goods, which was to change women's domestic role. Although Mary Crawford, with her London ways, speaks sarcastically of "the sweets of housekeeping in a country village", it is clear where Jane Austen's preferences lie. The self-sufficiency of a large estate or farm is her ideal. Even more modest households, such as those of the clergy, were capable of cultivating most of their own food. The work associated with all this was unremitting, calling for intelligence and good judgement. Performed well, it gave women a valuable role in society and a sense of self-worth.

Health and home remedies

MARTHA, LADY AUSTEN, SECOND WIFE OF JANE'S BROTHER FRANK. AS MARTHA LLOYD SHE KEPT A BOOK OF HOME REMEDIES.

AMONG THE SKILLS that Georgian women had to cultivate was that of nursing and doctoring their own families. Although most middle-class families had access to a professional medical man from the nearest large village or town, his services were of doubtful efficacy and would only have been called upon in serious cases.

Childbirth

Doctors did not become involved in childbirth until the latter part of the nineteenth century. A "monthly nurse" was sometimes hired to assist in the delivery and attend the mother during the month of her confinement, but very often the whole business was managed by a female relation. Three of Jane Austen's brothers lost their first wives in childbirth; for two of them, it was their eleventh confinement. Mothers could die at the birth itself; or they could appear to make a good recovery, only to be struck down a week or more after the birth by puerperal fever, caused by infection getting into the womb. This was the fate of Edward's wife Elizabeth.

Rather than breast-feed their children themselves, it was the habit of upper-class women to employ a wet-nurse. Of course there was no contraception. "I am quite tired of so many children," wrote Jane Austen, on hearing of someone's thirteenth pregnancy. After another birth, she recommended the couple adopt "the simple regimen of separate rooms".

Dentistry

A smaller consumption of sugar probably meant less decay. On the other hand, it is known that Mrs Austen had lost her front teeth by the time she was forty, probably from a mild form of scurvy caused by lack of fresh produce in the winter months, especially before potatoes became commonplace in the diet. Dentists were only found in the larger cities. Harriet Smith has to go to London when a tooth is amiss, as did two of Jane's nieces, there being no dentist in a town even the size of Canterbury. No dentists are listed in the Bath Guide of 1790, but by 1800 there were four. Dental work must have been excruciating before the invention of anaesthetics.

Martha Lloyd's household book

Jane and Cassandra's friend Martha Lloyd, who shared their home at Chawton and who, in middle age, married their brother Frank as his second wife, collected recipes of both the edible and medicinal kind, writing them into a leather-bound volume. Her home remedies are particularly interesting because of the ailments they purported to cure. There are remedies here for, among other complaints: colds;

sore eyes; worms; the staggers; pain in the side; gravel; fever; toothache; ague; consumption; and the bite of a mad dog. Martha's remedies are so weird and wonderful that one feels she would have been taken for a witch in an earlier epoch. The seasons of the moon figure in some of her prescriptions. For "hooping cough", a complaint which Jane suffered at the age of thirty, Martha's advice is:

> *Cut off the hair from the top of the head as large as a crown piece. Take a piece of brown paper of the same size: dip it in rectified oyl of amber, and apply it to the part for nine mornings, dipping the paper fresh every morning. If the cough is not remov'd try it again after three or four days.*

Oil of amber and the various other strange ingredients required by Martha's recipes would have been purchased from a druggist's shop. So would a very common home remedy which Jane Austen mentions twice in her letters and once in *Northanger Abbey*: rhubarb, taken for a disordered stomach. This is not the stalks we eat as fruit but the rootstock of the species of rheum grown in China and Tibet, imported at great expense into Europe, and available at a cost of about 3 shillings (15 new pence) per ounce. Also obtainable from the druggist were the smelling salts, or carbonate of ammonia, that many women carried about with them to meet all eventualities. When Louisa Musgrove falls from the Cobb, Anne Elliot can immediately produce salts; so can Mrs Jennings at a dinner party when Marianne burst into tears. Aromatic vinegar and lavender water, also used as revivors in the novels, could be made at home.

The Bath Cure

When home remedies failed and country apothecaries could do no better, many sufferers resorted to "taking the waters" at Bath, and later, at other watering-places, inland and by the sea. Several characters in the novels are ordered to Bath for a gouty constitution, as was Jane Austen's own uncle Leigh Perrot, who spent half of every year in the city, religiously drinking the water twice a day. Not only gout but lameness, infertility, diseases of the skin and of the digestive system were, it was claimed by the medical profession, curable by the waters of Bath, internally or externally taken. In 1800 there were 18 surgeons, 23 physicians, 28 apothecaries and "chymists" in the city. There were obviously rich pickings for medical men among the desperate invalids who flocked to Bath. One such invalid was Edward's mother-in-law Lady Bridges, who spent the winter of 1814–15 in Bath. "Dr Parry wished it," reported Jane, "not from thinking the water necessary to Lady B – but that he might be better able to judge how far his treatment of her, which is totally different from anything she is used to – is right; and I suppose he will not mind having a few more of her ladyship's guineas. His system is a lowering one. He took twelve ounces of Blood from her when the Gout appeared, & forbids wine, etc." The expensive Dr Parry or the homely Martha Lloyd – there does not seem much to choose between their cures. In Jane Austen's day, whether one recovered from an illness was down to little more than luck.

Martha Lloyd's cure for "a swell'd neck"

The day the moon is full a gentle dose of salts should be taken, and then the next day take 20 grains of burnt spunge in honey, syrop or anything that will mix with it; every morning fasting till the moon changes. Then take another gentle dose of salts and leave off till the moon is full again; and so on for a considerable time until benefit is found.

TAKING THE CURE AT BATH. THE WATERS RISE AT A TEMPERATURE OF 48° C.

A Little Education

THE AUSTENS WERE UNUSUAL in sending their daughters to school while teaching their sons at home. In most families the boys would have had the advantage of any money that was to be spent on education. Mr Austen was such a fine teacher that it made sense for him to teach his sons. Mild-mannered as well as learned, he inspired enduring affection in his pupils. Meanwhile his daughters went for short periods to two different boarding schools, but from the age of eleven Jane's only education was acquired from the books in her father's library, and the conversation of her parents and brothers.

ST JOHNS COLLEGE, OXFORD, ATTENDED BY JANE AUSTEN'S FATHER AND TWO OF HER BROTHERS. ELIZA AUSTEN WISHED SHE COULD BE A FELLOW AND WALK IN THE GARDENS EVERY DAY.

Male education

Boys were educated either privately in their own home by a tutor, or in the home of a gentleman scholar like Mr Austen, or at one of the public schools. Edward Knight's six sons went to Winchester College, as did their cousin James Edward, only son of James Austen. In the novels, Henry Crawford is a pupil at Westminster School, the Bertram sons at Eton. Their education consisted principally of Latin and Greek, with some arithmetic. James and Henry Austen were the only two of Jane's brothers to go to university. They were members of their father's old college, St John's, Oxford, but whereas he had won a scholarship from Tonbridge School, they had their fees paid under the rule of Founder's Kin. This archaic custom offered a free education to any boy who could prove he was descended from the original benefactor of the college, in this case Sir Thomas White, from whom Mrs Austen could trace descent. The rule was intended to compensate heirs for the money that had been lost to the family by the act of founding the college; but as the generations passed it was growing more and more indefensible, and was abolished in the reforms of the nineteenth century.

Another aspect of eighteenth century male education was the Grand Tour, undertaken either after university or – as in the case of Jane's brother Edward – instead of it. Under this system, a young man spent a year or two travelling on the Continent, perhaps in the care of a tutor, acquiring culture and languages and paying particular attention to the remains of antiquity. Edward's travels were paid for by his benefactor Thomas Knight, but even his poorer brothers, James and Henry, managed to spend some time in France between university and settling down to a career.

Female education

Needless to say, female education was much more limited and *ad hoc*. Most girls of the period were educated at home, perhaps by a governess, or more often simply by their mothers. We know about the education of all Jane Austen's heroines except Elinor and Marianne Dashwood. The Bennet girls have been left to acquire whatever education they can at home. Lady Catherine is quite shocked that no governess was provided for them: "Your mother must have been quite a slave to your education" she exclaims in horror. We are as amused as Elizabeth by the idea. "We were always encouraged to read, and had all the masters that were necessary. Those who chose to be idle, certainly might," she says. By masters, she means men who visited the house to impart such accomplishments as drawing, dancing and music.

The first chapter of *Northanger Abbey* describes Catherine Morland's education at home. "Writing and accounts she was taught by her father; French by her mother", these lessons coming to an end by the age of ten. During her teenage years she is left to her own devices, reading whatever she likes in a desultory fashion. The other female education we hear of in detail is that provided by the governess Miss Lee at Mansfield Park. She instructs the Bertram sisters how to "put the map of Europe together" and to repeat "the chronological order of the kings of England, with the dates of their accession, and most of the principal events of their reigns" as well as a list of "the Roman emperors as low as Severus; besides a great deal of the Heathen Mythology, and all the Metals, Semi-Metals, Planets, and distinguished philosophers".

It is clear that Jane Austen does not have much time for such superficial acquirements. Although Miss Lee teaches Fanny Price French, and hears her read "the daily portion of History", it is Edmund who guides her reading and forms her taste. Emma, being motherless, is taught by the governess who is like a mother to her, Miss Taylor. When Anne Elliot's mother dies, she is sent to school in Bath, an unhappy period for her. Girls' schools, in fact, seem often to have served this purpose, of getting girls out of the way. Mrs Goddard's school in Highbury, for example, standing in high repute, is a place where "girls might be sent to be out of the way and scramble themselves into a little education, without any danger of coming back prodigies".

ATTENTED BY JANE AND CASSANDRA, THE ABBEY GATE SCHOOL WAS KEPT BY MRS LATOURNELLE.

The teaching profession

Either as governess or schoolmistress, this was the only occupation open to an educated woman who had to make her own living. Mrs Goddard, as owner of a school, has earned a respectable place for herself in the local community, but the three teachers who assist her have no social status in Highbury; they are never included in invitations. Jane Fairfax, about to embark on a life as a governess, likens it to slavery. And in the unfinished fragment known as *The Watsons*, there is this exchange between two sisters:

"I would rather be a Teacher at a school (and I can think of nothing worse) than marry a Man I did not like."

"I would rather do anything than be Teacher at a school," said her sister. *I* have been at school, Emma, and know what a life they lead – *you* never have."

"GOODY TWO-SHOES" A CHILDREN'S BOOK OWNED BY JANE AUSTEN.

The Accomplished Woman

ACCOMPLISHMENTS FORMED an essential part of an upper or middle class woman's education. Their purpose was not to bring pleasure and improvement to herself, though of course that was sometimes the case. Rather they were embellishments to increase her attractiveness to potential marriage partners and to make her an asset in social gatherings.

In *Pride and Prejudice* there is a lively debate about what constitutes the truly accomplished woman. Charles Bingley thinks all the young ladies of his acquaintance are accomplished; but he is easily satisfied, since his idea of accomplishment is nothing more than painting tables, covering screens and netting purses. His sister is more rigorous:

A woman must have a thorough knowledge of music, singing, drawing, dancing and the modern languages to deserve the word; and besides all this, she must possess a certain something in her air and manner of walking, the tone of her voice, her address and expressions, or the word will be but half deserved.

Doubtless Miss Bingley imagines she is describing herself. But Darcy also demands of the accomplished woman "something more substantial, in the improvement of her mind by extensive reading".

PAINTING BY CASSANDRA OF A LADY WITH A MUSICAL INSTRUMENT. BOTH MUSIC AND ART WERE PRIZED FEMALE ACCOMPLISHMENTS.

A choice of accomplishments

Darcy is exceptional in having such high standards. As Miss Bingley's definition suggests, the usual accomplishments were playing a musical instrument, singing and drawing.

We have seen how the Bennet girls were provided with visiting masters in some or all of these arts. Catherine Morland, too, is taught the piano for a year between the ages of eight and nine by a visiting master. But she dislikes it and her kindly, pragmatic mother does not insist on her daughters being accomplished against their will. "The day which dismissed the music-master was one of the happiest of Catherine's life."

The parents of girls who were educated at school would have to pay extra for these lessons, again almost certainly from visiting masters. The number of accomplishments therefore reflected the financial standing of the family, and how much sacrifice they were prepared to make to improve their daughters' chances of marrying well.

Sometimes sisters divided the standard accomplishments between them, according to aptitude. Jane Austen played the piano, her sister drew. In *Sense and Sensibility*, Marianne plays and Elinor draws. Among the Bennet girls, Elizabeth plays and sings though not particularly well because she will not practise; Mary practises assiduously, but with her it is to compensate for being the only plain one in the family.

Emma Woodhouse is another young lady who will not practise as much as she ought, but she has the rudiments of both drawing and playing the piano. Anne Elliot can play well and, uniquely among the heroines, she has some knowledge of Italian. Henrietta and Louisa Musgrove have been taught the harp at school. The harp seems to have been more fashionable than the piano. Mary Crawford plays it exquisitely, and if Jane Fairfax could only teach the harp as well as the piano, according to Mrs Elton, she could, as governess, name her own terms. No accomplishments have been paid for as part of Harriet Smith's education. She cannot play the piano – but she can dance, as can all the young ladies in the novels.

Dancing lessons were essential for everybody who had any pretensions at all to social life. To take an example from real life, the only accomplishment thought necessary for Martha Lloyd and her two sisters – friends and contemporaries of Jane Austen, and like her daughters of a clergyman – was dancing. All the rest of their rather meagre education was imparted by their mother, but dancing and deportment Mrs Lloyd did consider "essential to the condition of a gentlewoman". So, for several years, "They were sent early in the day once a week to Mrs Hutchin's school, where the dancing master Mr Dore gave his attendance. It was a whole day of dancing. They began in the morning, stayed and dined with the schoolgirls, had another dancing lesson in the evening, and after tea the carriage fetched them home." This took place in the 1780s.

The use and abuse of accomplishments

When accomplishments were used to flaunt the wealth and status of the family, or to elevate the daughters above the condition of the parents, Jane Austen is severe upon them, as she is when they are too obviously designed as husband-baits. Miss Bingley stands arraigned on both counts. So does Augusta Hawkins, who becomes Mrs Elton. That her boasted love of music is no more than a display to catch a husband is evident from her determination to neglect her music once she has secured him. All her married friends have done the same. This is not, of course, to suggest that Jane Austen despises accomplishments themselves, when they give girls and women the personal satisfaction of becoming proficient at an art. Elinor and Marianne are praised for the way they "employ themselves" with their chosen art forms. Anne Elliot is the very picture of a cultivated woman whose acquirements are ignored by others but give pleasure to herself. Nor does Jane Austen cavil at the pleasure derived by men from being in company with young lady performers. "You and Miss Fairfax gave us some very good music," says Mr Knightley to Emma; "I do not know a more luxurious state than sitting at one's ease to be entertained a whole evening by two such young women; sometimes with music and sometimes with conversation." We can always trust Mr Knightley's judgement; contributing to the sum of happiness of those about them was the most worthy of motivations for women to acquire accomplishments.

GEORGIANA DARCY AND ELIZABETH BENNET AT THE PIANO.

Needlework

NEEDLEWORK WAS SUCH an habitual occupation for women of the period that they referred to it simply as "work". There was plain sewing, the making and mending of clothes for themselves or others; and fancy work, decorative items of various kinds requiring a range of techniques. As a general rule, plain sewing would be undertaken in the privacy of the family; fancy work could be taken up and its progress displayed in front of visitors.

Sewing had its uses besides the obvious ones. The modest posture of bent head and delicate finger movements involved could be, in male eyes, a great enhancer of female charms. For a woman, a piece of needlework could prove a godsend in awkward situations. Fanny Price can quite properly refuse to lift her eyes from her sewing when Henry Crawford is attempting to engage her interest. Even the more self-confident heroine Elizabeth Bennet, when confused by Darcy's sudden appearance at Hunsford Parsonage, "sat down again to her work, with an eagerness which it did not often command".

Dressmaking

Gowns, pelisses and other garments requiring a good fit would usually be made up to the customer's requirements by a professional seamstress who might come to the house for fittings. In 1811, Jane Austen mentions a Miss Burton who charged 8 shillings (40p) for making up a pelisse. But since, except for the very rich, clothes had to last a long time, Jane Austen and her friends frequently altered their clothes themselves to conform to the latest fashions. For example, Jane writes of adding a flounce to lengthen a skirt, and different trimmings to give clothes a new lease of life. Lesser items such as underwear, nightwear, caps, children's clothes and men's shirts, would all be made at home.

When Fanny visits her Portsmouth family, her young brother Sam is just about to go to sea for the first time. Anxious to be useful, Fanny "set about working for Sam immediately, and by working early and late, with perseverance and great despatch, did so much, that the boy was shipped off at last, with more than half his linen ready." Part of the skill lay in cutting out the fabric, since there were no paper patterns to be bought. At Mansfield Park itself, it is Lady Bertram's maid who makes her a new dress for the ball. But a greater number of servants to help did not mean the ladies of the house need be idle. "If you have no work of your own, I can supply you from the poor-basket," Mrs Norris admonishes Fanny. The custom of sewing clothes for the poor, particularly baby clothes, was quite a common one.

Embroidery and fancy work

Particularly popular at this period was white embroidery on white muslin, perhaps at the neck, sleeves or hem of a gown. Tambour work was a special form of embroidery in chain stitch done with a hook rather than a needle and using a tambour frame over which the muslin to be worked was stretched. Mrs Grant in *Mansfield Park* is the owner of a tambour frame. Embroidery in coloured silks was used to make pictures and samplers. Tapestry, or carpet-work as it is referred to in several of the novels, is cross-stitch in silk or wool on a canvas ground, and was used for upholstery, hangings and rugs.

Other techniques were knotting, netting and

knitting, though the last seems to have been the preserve of very old ladies, like Mrs Bates in *Emma*. Netting was more fashionable. Using a kind of shuttle, linen, cotton, silk or woollen thread was formed into an open net fabric, which could be used as an over-layer for cloaks, gowns and purses. Netting tools and materials were kept in special netting-boxes. Both Catherine Morland and Fanny Price own such an item.

Knotting also involved the use of a shuttle to knot the thread at intervals, forming a narrow trimming that looked rather like a row of beads. This could be couched to a fabric as part of an embroidered decoration, or used in the form of fringe on curtains, rugs and shawls. Lady Bertram, sitting on her sofa, makes yards and yards of fringe.

Jane Austen and sewing

Jane Austen did not despise these female arts. On the contrary, she took pride and pleasure in her handiwork, and applied the same high standards to the productions of her needle as to those of her pen. "I am the neatest worker of the party," she was once pleased to confess; and in another context, "An artist cannot do anything slovenly".

Several examples of her needlework survive to prove that these were no idle boasts. One is a delicately embroidered white lawn handkerchief that she made for Cassandra. There is a different motif, white on white, in each corner, one of which incorporates the initials CA. Another item is a muslin shawl embroidered all over with a trellis pattern in satin stitch.

There is also a patchwork quilt made by Jane, Cassandra and their mother in about 1811. Diamond-shaped pieces of floral chintz are surrounded by smaller patches of black and white spotted cotton. All these are on display in the Chawton museum, as is a small needle-book made by Jane Austen to encourage a niece just beginning to learn to sew.

PATCHWORK QUILT MADE BY JANE AUSTEN, MRS AUSTEN AND CASSANDRA.

THE NEEDLE CASE – THE WRAPPING PAPER SAYS "WITH AUNT JANE'S LOVE."

Music

MUSIC PLAYED AN IMPORTANT part in the social lives of Jane Austen's people. This was despite – or perhaps because of – the absence of recorded, instantly available music, which is one of the greatest differences between their time and our own. For us, it is unimaginable not to have music on tap. For them, to hear music played professionally was a rarity, and if they wished their lives to be enhanced by music, they had to work hard at learning and performing it themselves.

JANE AUSTEN'S MUSIC BOOK, TRANSCRIBED IN HER OWN HAND.

Professional music

For both Jane Austen and her characters, opportunities to hear professional music were mainly confined to London and Bath. In London, besides regular public concerts, it was possible to hire professional musicians for performances in private homes. This is what Henry and Eliza did one evening in 1811 when Jane happened to be staying with them. More than eighty guests were invited to a musical soirée with five professional musicians, including a harpist. The harp seems to have been Jane Austen's favourite musical experience; singing her least favourite. On a later visit to London Jane accompanied Henry to an opera, Thomas Arne's *Artaxerxes*, a musical experience that she did not enjoy.

The city of Bath had an equally active musical life. On Wednesday evenings throughout the season, subscription concerts took place at the Upper Rooms under the direction of the celebrated Signor Rauzzini. Catherine Morland and all her acquaintance attend the Wednesday concerts as a matter of course. The Elliots, in *Persuasion*, go less frequently into public, but they do patronise one concert at the Upper Rooms, complete with Italian songs. The Bath season ended about May, but in the summer months occasional concerts would be held out of doors in Sydney Gardens.

Music at home

These events in the life and novels are the exceptions. Most of the music in Jane Austen's world is home-grown, like the stirring piano concertos produced by Marianne Dashwood, or the harp-playing with which Mary Crawford delights first Edmund and then Fanny. In fact the novels are full of lady performers, some who have a genuine love of music, others who simply crave the attention it brings.

It is noticeable that it is the female half of the population who produce the music. The man's role is to listen, appreciate and admire. No gentleman in any of the novels plays an instrument. Some of them sing, but only in a duet with a lady – Frank Churchill and Jane Fairfax, for example – or in a mixed-group glee, such as that which collects the Bertrams and the Crawfords round the piano at Mansfield Park.

The only solo male singer in the novels is Robert Martin's shepherd's son, who has a sweet voice, and who is called in to the parlour at Abbey Mill Farm one evening for Harriet's pleasure. The boy, of course, belongs to the lower orders, as does the unnamed violinist who chances to be in the servants' hall at Mansfield Park one evening, and is the cause of an impromptu little ball. Certainly, male musicians are seen in the light of "hirelings" – to use Jane Austen's term; the inference is that no gentleman learns to play an instrument unless he needs to make a living from it. The opposite is the case with ladies. For them to play enhances their claims to good breeding.

Jane Austen, pianist

Jane was the musical one of the two sisters and therefore, since music was so much a female preserve, the only provider of music in the Austen household. She played the piano with a high degree of competence, taking lessons from a visiting master at least until the age of twenty-one. Her teacher, George William Chard, assistant organist at Winchester Cathedral at the time of Jane's lessons, eventually became Master of Music at Winchester College, so we may suppose he was a good teacher. As a young man he supplemented his income by visiting pupils in their homes; he had to travel fourteen miles for Jane's lessons, paid for by by Mr Austen.

When the family left Steventon Jane's piano had to be sold. It was her own property, and she received eight guineas for it. Eight years later, on settling at Chawton, one of her first thoughts was to have a piano again, even though the price of them seems to have risen, and the family were less well off than they had been:

> *Yes, yes, we will have a pianoforte, as good a one as can be got for thirty guineas, and I will practise country dances, that we may have some amusement for our nephews and nieces, when we have the pleasure of their company.*

She did practise most mornings for an hour before breakfast, when she could feel she was not disturbing anybody else. Perhaps her pleasure was as much in the opportunity to be alone, and to lose herself in her thoughts, as in the sounds she was making. Like her own Anne Elliot, she could let her mind wander "while her fingers were mechanically at work, proceeding for half an hour together, equally without error and without consciousness". Jane also made a collection of sheet music, copied neatly in her own hand, complete with index, which is still preserved at Chawton cottage, evidence that she took her role as the family's provider of music seriously.

SYDNEY GARDENS IN BATH WHERE JANE AUSTEN ATTENDED PUBLIC CONCERTS.

DRAWING ROOM AT CHAWTON COTTAGE WITH A PIANO DATING C.1810.

Dancing

JANE AUSTEN LOVED DANCING. There are frequent references to it in her letters, for example this written when she was twenty: "We had an exceedingly good ball last night … There were twenty dances, and I danced them all, without any fatigue."

Considering that it was one of the few forms of physical exercise which could be indulged in by women, that it gave an excuse for wearing one's best clothes and ornaments and showing off how gracefully one could move, as well as opportunity for meeting new people, for flirting and even serious courtship, the popularity of dancing among women of Jane Austen's class is hardly surprising.

CHILDREN LEARNING TO DANCE THE QUADRILLE.

Balls and dances

The most prestigious kind of ball was that which took place at a great country house. It would be planned some time in advance, invitations sent out to all the neighbouring gentry, professional musicians engaged, and an elaborate supper laid on. In the novels, such balls are given by Sir Thomas Bertram at Mansfield Park and Charles Bingley at Netherfield. From Steventon, the Austens attended even grander balls held by the aristocrats Lord Portsmouth and Lord Bolton. As local leaders of society, they would dispense this kind of hospitality perhaps once every year or two years in a spirit of benevolent condescension. Their neighbours were expected to return to their respective stations in life when the fun was over.

At the other end of the scale was the impromptu dance held after dinner in an ordinary house, with family and a few friends. At the suggestion probably of the young people, the furniture would be pushed back, one of the older women pressed into service to play the piano, and two or three couples would "stand up". It is this kind of dance, with Anne Elliot at the piano, which often closes the evening at Uppercross.

Public assemblies

Most of Jane Austen's opportunities for dancing occurred at the Basingstoke Assemblies. Between 1792, when she was old enough for dancing, and 1801, when the Austens left Hampshire, more than fifty such balls were held, through the winter months, at Basingstoke Town Hall. Here the older people of the neighbourhood could meet their acquaintance to talk and play cards, the young to dance, flirt and look for marriage partners. Despite the slightly uncontrolled social mix – for anyone who could afford the right clothes and transport could attend, the Basingstoke Assembly was occasionally honoured even by the Portsmouths and Boltons. In the same way, in *Pride and Prejudice*, Bingley's party honours the Meryton Assembley, at the "country town" tone of which Darcy turns up his nose.

Every town with pretensions to fashion and a sizeable middle-class population, either resident or

DANCING AT THE CLIFTON ASSEMBLY ROOMS, BRISTOL. THE ROOMS OPENED IN 1806, THE YEAR JANE AUSTEN STAYED IN CLIFTON.

visiting, had built itself an Assembly Room by this time. In Bath, to cater for the large number of visitors, there were two sets of rooms, in the Upper and Lower parts of the city. In *Northanger Abbey*, Catherine Morland finds the Upper Rooms so crowded that she can hardly move. This is in contrast to a ball attended there by Jane Austen herself toward the end of the season in 1801, when there were only twenty couples. "Rather thin for Bath," she reported to Cassandra, "though it would have made two or three pretty Basingstoke Assemblies".

In the Lower Rooms Catherine is introduced to Henry Tilney by the Master of Ceremonies. This job had once been graced by the famous "Beau" Nash, who had done so much to regulate polite behaviour earlier in the century. A nation of country bumpkins, coming together for pleasure at Bath, had been transformed into one of the most sophisticated societies ever known. It was this society which Jane Austen and her generation inherited.

The English country dance

In contrast to the ballroom dancing of the nineteenth and early twentieth centuries, in which couples twirl around more or less oblivious to what everyone else is doing, dancing in the eighteenth and early nineteenth century was a highly communal affair. All the dancers faced one another, their movements making stylized patterns in which observers could take aesthetic pleasure.

This style of dancing had originated in the French court, where a set number of dancers stood in a square or circle. When imported into the English country house, or Assembly Rooms, dances were adapted to suit the oblong shape of most ballrooms. "Longways for as many as will" became the instruction for what became known as the English Country Dance.

The rationale of this kind of dancing was to demonstrate the polish, elegance and decorum of eighteenth century manners. Sir William Lucas harks back to this sense of self-congratulation when he remarks to Darcy, "There is nothing like dancing after all. I consider it as one of the first refinements of polished societies," to which Darcy's reply is, "Every savage can dance". As an example of Darcy's arrogance this is excellent, but for once Sir William has right on his side. To learn and execute perfectly the steps of an English country dance, to be still when required and to move when required, to make polite conversation while remaining alert to the demands of the dance, required real skill. It was a skill worth acquiring. As screen dramatizations of the novels have shown, the mechanics of English Country dancing – taking a few steps, exchanging a few words, perhaps spoken over the shoulder or under an uplifted arm, was highly conducive to engaging the interest of the opposite sex.

Courtship

DANCING GAVE THE PERFECT OPPORTUNITY FOR FLIRTATION AND COURTSHIP.

THE SUBJECT OF ALL Jane Austen's novels is courtship. In this she was following a well-worn convention of her time. Increasingly through the eighteenth century, young people were exercising the right to choose their life partners on the basis of attraction and compatibility, rather than submit to marriages arranged by their elders for dynastic reasons. The novel itself as a literary form virtually sprang up in response to this change: for if lifelong personal happiness was to be staked on a complete stranger, the need to assess the characters of other people became vital. The courtship novel as a sub-genre was well established by Jane Austen's day. In lesser hands it was often trivial and hence derided by male commentators. But it suited Jane Austen's talents to perfection, affording her both scope for high comedy and an underlying seriousness of purpose.

Etiquette

The etiquette of courtship was designed to protect the woman's reputation and hence her value in the marriage market. Hers was a purely passive role. To respond to a man's attentions before his intentions were known was to risk the ridicule of other people or the pain of disappointment. So she must appear hardly to notice, and certainly to attach no significance to, male attentions until the moment of proposal. A model of such behaviour is Fanny Price, observed approvingly by her uncle:

> *Sir Thomas heard and was not offended. There was no want of respect in the young man's address; and Fanny's reception of it was so proper and modest, so calm and uninviting, that he had nothing to censure in her. She said little, assented only here and there, and betrayed no inclination . . . of appropriating any part of the compliment to herself.*

Those harsh words "censure" and "offended" show how seriously Sir Thomas – who stands for authority and decorum – regards any breach of etiquette in courtship.

Prohibitions

There was much behaviour prohibited to a young couple before they were engaged. This included using Christian names, unless connected by family; driving in carriages alone together; correspondence; exchanging gifts; and any kind of intimate touching. If any of these were observed to take place, then the automatic assumption was that the couple were engaged.

Marianne and Willoughby are guilty of all five kinds of transgression. He calls her Marianne; they drive to Allenham alone on the day the picnic is cancelled; she writes to him in London; he offers to give her a horse, which she enthusiastically accepts; and she allows him to cut off a lock of her hair. The catalogue of these transgressions is enough to indicate how close her unconventionality brings her to losing her honour.

It is innocence rather than unconventionality that betrays Catherine Morland into driving alone with John Thorpe. When she hears from Mr Allen – more alert to his duties as chaperone than his wife – that it is "not quite the thing", she is horrified at having committed such an error.

Because of the prohibition on touch, even permitted social touching could carry an erotic charge. This is the case when Mary Crawford accepts Edmund Bertram's offer of an arm to lean on while out walking, with Fanny making the essential third. "The gratification of having her do so, of feeling such a connection for the first time, made him a little forgetful of Fanny" not surprisingly. A similarly charged moment occurs when Mr Knightley takes Emma's hand, presses it, is on the point of carrying it to his lips, then stops – rather to her disappointment.

Since the courting couple could never be truly alone, the best they could hope for was to be out of earshot of the other people present. Country walks provided some of the best opportunities for private conversation, but even better was the dance floor. Under cover of music and with their elders ranged at some distance round the edges of the room, young people could talk, touch hands, and concentrate on one another in a way not permissible elsewhere.

The proposal

For the proposal itself, the man had to manoeuvre a private interview; that alone would signal his intention. Sometimes he would ask a parent's permission first, as Mr Collins does when he seeks Mrs Bennet's co-operation in getting Elizabeth by herself. Captain Wentworth can never detach Anne from her relations in Bath, so has recourse to a letter to open his campaign. When next they meet, she can answer him only with a look, until Charles Musgrove luckily remembers some urgent business in a shop, which leaves the lovers alone together for the first time in the book. But the funniest manoeuvring is actually performed by a woman, when Charlotte Lucas, spying Mr Collins from an upstairs window, "set out to meet him accidentally in the lane".

If a woman rejected a proposal, it was a point of honour to keep the man's failure to herself. A sister might be told, perhaps, but certainly not another man. Mr Knightley, guessing that Mr Elton once proposed to Emma, says with a smile, "To that surmise, you say nothing, of course". Whatever faults Emma Woodhouse has, she only once, on Box Hill, fails to act with perfect good breeding and in conformity with the etiquette of her times.

The artificiality of Mr Elton's style of courtship, with his charades and compliments and caution, is contrasted with that of Robert Martin, who plays no games with the object of his love, Harriet Smith, but who tries to please her out of the simplicity of his heart by calling in his shepherd boy to sing to her and by riding about the country gathering walnuts because she likes them. It is perhaps the most charming of any courtship in Jane Austen.

A charade

THE WORD COURTSHIP IS THE SOLUTION TO A CHARADE, WHICH THE INSINUATING MR ELTON CONTRIBUTES TO THE COLLECTION OF HARRIET AND EMMA:

My first displays the wealth and pomp of kings,
Lords of the earth! their luxury and ease.
Another view of man my second brings,
Behold him there, the monarch of the seas.
But ah! united, what reverse we have!
Man's boasted power and freedom, all are flown;
Lord of the earth and sea, he bends a slave,
And woman, lovely woman, reigns alone.

MR BINGLEY'S COURTSHIP OF JANE BENNET, DEFLECTED FOR A WHILE BY HIS SISTERS AND MR DARCY.

Verse and Theatricals

FAMILIES WITH LITERARY TASTES, like the Austens, passed many of their leisure hours in verbal pursuits, which exercised their powers of fun and invention. Besides reading aloud, they enjoyed composing light verse for their own and each other's amusement and, for a period in Jane's childhood, the whole family were swept up in a passion for amateur theatricals.

Light verse

It was Mrs Austen who brought the habit of writing light verse into the family. She and her brother James Leigh Perrot had both practised this minor but by no means easy art since childhood, and the Austen children were encouraged to try their hand. Sometimes in the evening circle it would be a communal activity, as on the occasion when everyone present tried writing a poem every line of which rhymed with "rose". On such occasions, Mrs Austen's was invariably the wittiest contribution, with Jane's a close second.

More often, an individual would be inspired by some incident or piece of news into writing a stanza or two of lively nonsense. A good example is the following by Jane Austen:

POPULAR IN THEIR DAY, AMATEUR THEATRICALS APPEAR IN "MANSFIELD PARK".

ON READING IN THE NEWSPAPERS
THE MARRIAGE OF
MR GELL TO MISS GILL,
OF EASTBOURNE

At Eastbourne Mr Gell,
From being perfectly well,
Became dreadfully ill,
For love of Miss Gill.
So he said, with some sighs,
I'm the slave of your iis;
Oh, restore, if you please,
By accepting my ees.

Mrs Austen was even capable of passing on a recipe in verse; and the lines she wrote on recovering from a serious illness in Bath are as full of feeling as they are of humour. Jane Austen, too, only three days before her death, composed a poem about St Swithin and Winchester which is, in her brother's words, "replete with fancy and vigour".

None of Jane Austen's characters is given to this kind of composition. But then, she creates no family quite as clever and fun-loving as that into which she was so lucky to be born. The nearest thing in the novels is the collection of riddles and charades which Harriet Smith is copying neatly into a little home-made book – but a feeble shadow of the Austen practice. "In this age of literature," as Jane Austen remarks with heavy irony, "such collections on a very grand scale are not uncommon. Miss Nash, head teacher at Mrs Goddard's, had written out at least three hundred."

Amateur theatricals

There was a rage for amateur theatricals in the late eighteenth and early nineteenth centuries. It was introduced into the Austen household by the undergraduate son James. The first play produced by the family was in 1782, when Jane was in her seventh year; the last in January 1790, when she had just turned fourteen. Too young to be much more than a wide-eyed spectator and performer of minor parts, she turned her observations and reflections to good account twenty years later in the amateur theatrical episode in *Mansfield Park*.

At Steventon, plays were put on in the dining parlour at first, but as they became more ambitious, the barn was requisitioned. A cousin of the Austens reported at Christmas 1787, "My uncle's barn is fitting up quite like a theatre, & all the young folks are to take their part". With all the family gathering at Steventon, and more distant members invited to fill up the parts, another cousin wrote, "My aunt Austen declares 'She has not room for any idle young people' ".

The plays chosen were mainly eighteenth century trifles now largely forgotten, ranging from the tragedy *Matilda* to the comedy *High Life below Stairs*, though one year Sheridan's comic masterpiece *The Rivals* was put on. Characteristically, the Austen input was not confined to acting and production. James, the most literary member of the family, until Jane's abilities began to ripen, wrote prologues and epilogues to all the plays performed. It was when James left home to become a staid married clergyman that the rage for acting at Steventon came to an end.

Whatever went on "behind the scenes" at Steventon – and there is a suggestion that cousin Eliza used acting as an excuse for flirting with both James and Henry at once – as a novelist Jane Austen clearly saw the narrative potential of bringing a group of young people together in this slightly artificial environment, when some of the usual decorum governing social life could be put aside. In *Mansfield Park*, acting encourages showing off and selfishness of various kinds. The pleasure that the characters hope to achieve from the theatricals turns sour for almost them all. As a device for illustrating the interplay of character, the play chosen is so perfect that one wonders which came first for Jane Austen: the creation of the Bertrams and the Crawfords – or the choice of *Lovers' Vows*.

ELIZA DE FEUILLIDE, WHO USED THE AMATEUR THEATRICALS AT STEVENTON TO FLIRT WITH HER COUSINS.

Games of skill and chance

WITH MANY LEISURE HOURS to fill and no ready-made entertainment, indoor games were a regular feature of social and family life. Card games, word games and games of manual dexterity were all popular in Jane Austen's day, and a great number of different ones are referred to in the novels and letters. Many of these games are no longer familiar today.

Depending on the mentality of the players, games could be dull and ponderous, or highly entertaining. In the novels, it is the charming and intelligent Henry Crawford who brings to cards "all the lively turns, quick resources, and playful impudence that could do honour to the game", but it is easy to imagine the Austen family playing with similar spirit. When Jane was obliged to endure her aunt Leigh Perrot's staid card parties in Bath, however, it was another story. "Another stupid party," she reported, using the word as we would use "stupifying", meaning enough to send one to sleep.

Card games

Commerce, cribbage, speculation, vingt-un and whist are the card games mentioned in Jane Austen's letters. Commerce also appears in *Pride and Prejudice* and *Northanger Abbey*, where it is played, suitably enough, by the mercenary Isabella Thorpe. Other games in *Pride and Prejudice* include casino, whist, vingt-un, loo, quadrille and piquet. Cribbage, whist and speculation are mentioned in *Mansfield Park*, the latter game given symbolic meaning by Mary Crawford, who declares, "I will stake my last like a woman of spirit ... If I lose the game, it shall not be from not striving for it." Lose it she does.

It is evident from the novels that cards are played chiefly for the enjoyment of men. At Mansfield Parsonage the whist table is formed after tea: "formed really for the amusement of Dr Grant, by his attentive wife, though it was not to be supposed so", while at Netherfield Miss Bingley, as hostess, panders to her brother-in-law's taste for cards on two consecutive evenings and only declines his "open petition" on the third evening because she knows Darcy does not wish to play. At public and private balls, a card-room was always provided for the husbands and fathers who had no interest in the dancing, whist being the usual game. At the Mansfield Park ball, Mrs Norris is much occupied in making up whist tables. Rarely, however, were the men joined by the women of their own age, whose place was to sit round the edge of the ballroom, in chatting and observing the young people.

In public places gambling had been illegal since the middle of the eighteenth century, but at home cards were usually played for money. Even at Hartfield Mrs Goddard expects to win or lose "a few sixpences" in play with Mr Woodhouse, and at Netherfield Elizabeth suspects the company of "playing high". Doubtless this is one of the reasons why cards were Jane Austen's least favourite type of game. She once lost three shillings (60p) on a single game of commerce, remarking "I cannot afford to lose that twice in one

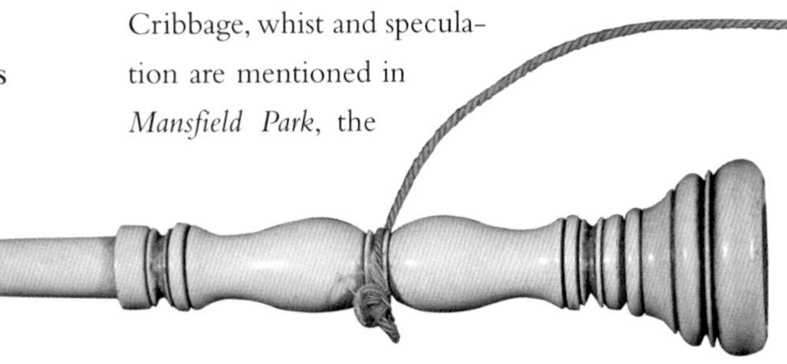

CUP AND BALL, WHICH BELONGED TO JANE AUSTEN. SHE EXCELLED AT GAMES OF DEXTERITY.

evening". She had other reasons for thinking cards inimical to social harmony. People were apt to take them too seriously, like Mrs Norris and Dr Grant in *Mansfield Park*, who can never play at cards without becoming disputatious. Others use cards to avoid the effort of conversation, like the vacuous Mr Hurst in *Pride and Prejudice*, who lives "only to eat, drink and play at cards".

Word games

Charades and riddles, played by the Austens, are two kinds of puzzle in rhyme. With charades, the word to be guessed is split into its component syllables. Riddles are rhymes to which the answer is a single word, or even a single letter of the alphabet. Many of these Austen family compositions have been preserved.

There are few word games in the novels except for Emma, where an abundance of games reflects the imaginative and manipulative nature of the heroine herself. In one episode, the characters make hidden words with Emma's nephews' "alphabets" – that is, pieces of card each bearing a hand-written letter. Later, Frank attempts to elicit verbal wit from the company on Box Hill, and succeeds with his father, who produces a conundrum on the name of Emma. Not to be outdone, Mrs Elton boasts that her own name was once the subject of an acrostic – a rhyme in which the initial letters of the lines spell out a word. Riddles and charades, of course, figure largely in Harriet's collection.

Other games

When the weather prevented field sports, the men of the house often resorted to billiards. There was a billiard table at Godmersham, and Jane Austen places them also at Cleveland and at Mansfield Park, both very masculine establishments.

Mr Woodhouse's favourite game is backgammon; Emma has to devote many an evening to this game, which was something like draughts, with counters, well suited to Mr Woodhouse's slow intellect, but offering little challenge to Emma.

Jane Austen herself excelled at games of manual dexterity, like nines, spillikins and bilbocatch, or cup and ball. These were really children's games, but she regarded the equipment required to play them as essential to any household, and enjoyed playing them when her nephews and nieces came to visit. The most energetic games she mentions playing with the younger generation are battledore and shuttlecock, but in *Northanger Abbey* the young Catherine Morland loves cricket and baseball, even though these are "boys' plays".

WALNUT GAMES TABLE C. 1710. THE TOP REVERSES FOR BACKGAMMON, CHESS OR CRIBBAGE.

Travel

JANE AUSTEN'S LIFETIME coincided with the discovery by the leisured classes of travelling purely for pleasure. Until the last quarter of the eighteenth century, unnecessary journeys were rarely undertaken. Men might travel about by horseback on business, goods were transported across the country in lumbering wagons, or by water, but the only journeys whole families were liable to make were from their country estates to Bath or London and back. Even such journeys were confined to the richest level of society. Travelling was costly, uncomfortable and slow. Most people never went further than their nearest market town.

Improvements in the surfaces of the roads, paid for by the turnpike system of tolls, began to make journeys quicker and more comfortable toward the end of the century, as did corresponding improvements in the design and springing of carriages. At the same time, an increase in the general prosperity of the population meant that people in the middle reaches of society began to have sufficient money to spend on luxuries like travel.

THE STAGECOACH WAS THE LEAST ACCEPTABLE FORM OF TRAVEL FOR LADIES.

There was a third factor involved in the rage for travel. When Daniel Defoe had journeyed about Britain in the 1720s, his account centred on the varieties of local industry and agriculture he had encountered. This was interesting enough to readers who had never ventured beyond their own region. But it was not enough to make them brave the difficulties of travel themselves. A quite different emphasis emerged in the 1770s and 1780s with the books of William Gilpin, who reported on the natural beauties of different parts of the British Isles. Suddenly a desire to travel for the sake of what was to be seen was created in the literate public, in none more so than the Austens.

Long-distance travel

Most of the comfortably-off families in Jane Austen's novels keep their own carriage, as did even the Austens themselves in their Steventon days. The most prestigious way to travel was in one's own carriage. This could be drawn by either two or four horses, depending on whether speed or economy was the primary consideration. For journeys above about twenty miles, only the first stage of a journey could be done with the family's own horses, after which fresh ones had to be hired at posting inns along the route. An alternative was to give the horses a rest of about two hours, as General Tilney does at the Petty France inn between Bath and Northanger.

If the family did not possess its own carriage, it was possible to hire what was known as a hack chaise. Because of the difficulty of getting it back to its owner, usually the hired vehicle as well as the horses would be changed at each posting inn, involving frequent removals of luggage. This is how Catherine Morland, ejected from Northanger Abbey, and travelling quite alone, is obliged to make a journey of eleven hours from Gloucestershire to Wiltshire.

The lowliest form of transport was on the public stagecoach. Acceptable for men travelling alone, this was rarely resorted to by gentlewomen, though Jane herself did travel that way on at least one occasion, from Chawton to London. When the

Steele sisters travel from Devon to London, they let everyone know that it was "not in the stage". The child Fanny Price travels from Portsmouth to London by stagecoach, under the care of a tradeswoman who happens to be making the same journey. Later in the novel, both William Price and Edmund Bertram, separately, go by mail coach. In every way, men had the advantage over women in terms of mobility. Jane Austen herself was often obliged to wait until it was convenient for a brother to escort her home from a family visit.

The perils of travel

Although carriages could be equipped with lights when night travel was really necessary, it was of course more unpleasant and dangerous to journey in the dark. Wherever possible, social engagements were arranged for moonlit nights.

The seventeen mile journey from Uppercross to Lyme and back, in November, has to be spread over two days. In summer longer travelling hours were of course possible, but the Austens were accustomed to taking two days to travel from Hampshire to Kent, or in the other direction, from Hampshire to Bath. On reasonably good roads, about seven miles an hour could be accomplished.

Even in daylight, accidents frequently occurred, especially on minor, rutted roads. A cousin of Jane Austen's was killed outright when the carriage she was in overturned. The loss of luggage, especially when the passengers were travelling by hack chaise, was another risk. Jane Austen's precious portable writing desk, containing her manuscripts, which went everywhere with her, was once put on to the wrong coach at an inn. The mistake was soon realized and she got it back. Fashionable people embarking on long visits must have required an enormous quantity of luggage. Trunks were fastened on to the carriage, hatboxes and parcels placed inside.

A permanent removal of house – which the Austens undertook several times – was a major undertaking. When they left Steventon for Bath the cost of taking their furniture with them was not worthwhile; they sold everything but their beds, and bought afresh. The Dashwoods moving from Sussex to Devon transport their furniture by sea, while the Elliots, who leave most of their furniture at Kellynch, use wagons to take what they need from Somerset to Bath. Despite all these difficulties and dangers, an enthusiasm for travel was established in a large swathe of the population during Jane Austen's lifetime. Not only did it have an effect on civility and manners, as people came into contact with one another, it also altered the very landscape itself, as places developed to accommodate and give pleasure to the influx of fashionable visitors.

THERE WAS A NEW FASHION FOR VISITING PLACES SUCH AS THE LAKE DISTRICT IN SEARCH OF PICTURESQUE SCENERY.

TURNPIKE AT DURDHAM DOWN, CLIFTON, BRISTOL.

CHAPTER THREE

Society and the Spirit of the Age

One of the most fascinating aspects of Jane Austen's life is its position on the cusp of two centuries, partaking something of the flavour of both. In many ways she was deeply imbued with the ideas of the eighteenth century; and yet she was ready to take on the challenges of the nineteenth, as her late novels, particularly *Persuasion* and the unfinished *Sanditon*, show. Centuries are of course artificial divisions, yet can often be meaningful ones. And not only to historians, but to the people alive at the time. There is a sense of new beginnings, new energy, new ideas; of old ideas and old customs disappearing, never to return. As the eighteenth century slipped into the nineteenth, the old way of life known in Britain for centuries was undergoing a process of evolution – sometimes of revolution – into the kind of modern society we ourselves are familiar with. Jane Austen responded to these changes with the alert perceptions, profound interest and ambivalent emotions we would expect in an intelligent woman who really cared about the welfare of her country.

One of the greatest influences upon Jane Austen was the war against France, which raged through most of her life. It has been said that the Napoleonic Wars play little part in her novels, which is true, as far as direct reference goes. But they played an enormous part in shaping her beliefs. To her, France was not just a military threat, but an ideological one. Under both the revolutionaries and the Emperor, France seemed to stand for terror and tyranny and excess, things which Britain had been mercifully free from for a century. Not just the home territories, but far-flung maritime empires, were at stake in the struggle between the two great nations. Jane Austen's attitude to the colonial ambitions of her country must be understood in this light. The question was not whether to colonize or to leave the native peoples to settle their own destinies. It was whether France or Britain would be the colonial power.

The New World, which would develop and improve on British traditions, was still in its infancy; the British would have laughed to be told they had anything to learn from the upstart. Even the relations between the classes, to modern eyes so iniquitous, did include enough social mobility to enable exceptional individuals to fulfil their potential, with benefit both to the arts and the sciences. Moreover it produced a reasonably homogeneous population, given a benevolent and humanitarian approach on the part of those with power over the lives of others. This is always Jane Austen's most anxious concern, from Mr Darcy's virtue as a landlord, to the self-contained community of Highbury in *Emma*, which functions, at its best, as Jane Austen would like to see society functioning. She never wanted to change the structure of society; what she advocated, was for every member of society to play their part with kindliness, unselfishness, intelligence and duty. By the end of the eighteenth century, society had reached a fruitful balance between stability and openness to new ideas. This was favourable both to artistic expression, witness Jane Austen and the great poets and thinkers like Mary Wollstonecraft, and to the ingenuity which fired the Industrial Revolution, that most cataclysmic of all changes in the British way of life. It was an exciting age in which to live.

The Royal Family

GEORGE III WHO WAS ON THE THRONE FOR THE WHOLE OF JANE AUSTEN'S LIFETIME.

FOLLOWING THE RELIGIOUS and constitutional upheavals of the seventeenth century, the Protestant Hanoverians had been firmly established on the throne of Great Britain for over sixty years when Jane Austen was born. They had easily seen off the final challenge to their power, by the Young Pretender Charles Edward Stuart, in 1745, thirty years before her birth.

Jane's whole life was encompassed by the long reign of George III, who succeeded his grandfather in 1760 and died in 1821, four years after her own death. From 1811, however, the King's insanity resulted in his eldest son becoming Prince Regent. The last years of Jane's life, and the publication of all her novels, consequently belong to the short but distinctive period known as the Regency.

The madness of King George

Known to his subjects as "Farmer George", King George III of Great Britain was never happier than when allowed to behave like an ordinary middle-class person. Fond of country pursuits and domestic life, frugal and chaste in habit, he was devoted to his rather dull German wife, Queen Charlotte, who had borne him fifteen children. Disliking London, the royal couple lived as much as possible at Windsor or Kew, which their daughters referred to as "The Nunnery".

The court of George III was irreproachably respectable, stiff and formal. The novelist Fanny Burney, who was Keeper of the Queen's Wardrobe for several years in the 1780s, has left a vivid picture in her diaries of the tedium and protocol that surrounded every aspect of life at court, though she became fond of both their majesties, who were personally very kind to her.

While the children were small, the royal household presented a model of family life; but the seven princes who reached adulthood rebelled against their father's morality. They turned out dissolute and spendthrift, running up great debts, acquiring mistresses and illegitimate children, eating and drinking to excess and plotting with politicians against their father. The worst offender was the one of whom most was expected, the eldest son, George, Prince of Wales, known in the family as "Prinny".

Another kind of trouble made its first appearance in 1788 when the King became mentally deranged. It is now believed that he was suffering from an hereditary metabolic disorder, porphyria, the symptoms of which include paralysis, pain and delirium, all experienced by the poor King. The treatments of the day were barbaric, including the use of the strait-jacket. Over the next twenty years the malady made several reappearances, frequently threatening to precipitate a political crisis, until in 1811 the Regency Act was finally passed and Prinny became Prince Regent. For the last ten years of his life George III lived in virtual isolation, his only remaining comfort playing the harpsichord, until he became deaf as well as blind.

The Prince Regent

George IV, as he was eventually to become, was a man of contrasts. He was totally self-indulgent, as incapable of curbing his spending as of governing his passions. Sexually, he was most comfortable with older, voluptuous women, preferably intelligent ones. He had a butterfly mind, always influenced by the last person he had spoken to. Yet no English monarch has been so cultivated and interested in the arts. His request that the next Jane Austen novel be dedicated to him is proof that despite the grossness of his habits and appearance, he was capable of discerning the moral beauty in literature that one might have supposed too delicate for his jaded palate. Nor was his request just a passing whim: he kept a set of the novels in each of his residences.

He was a great patron of the visual arts and of architecture. The Regent's Park area of London was created under his patronage, while his own favourite residence, the onion-domed Royal Pavilion in Brighton, remains a lasting memorial to this paradoxical prince.

In 1785 he went through a kind of marriage ceremony with the twice-widowed Catholic Mrs Maria Fitzherbert, but the marriage was invalid since it violated both the Royal Marriages Act and the Act of Settlement. Ten years later his debts had amounted to £630,000, a quite staggering sum when one thinks of the Austens living on £600 p.a., or of Mr Darcy being a wealthy landowner on £10,000 p.a. The Prince struck a bargain with his father. He would marry a German princess of his father's choosing if his debts were settled and his income was doubled.

THE PRINCE OF WALES, LATER GEORGE IV, IN A GILLRAY CARTOON OF 1792. HIS GROSS HABITS MADE HIM HATEFUL TO JANE AUSTEN.

The result was disastrous. The Prince and his bride, his hoydenish cousin Princess Caroline of Brunswick, who had never met before the wedding day, loathed each other on sight. They managed to conceive Princess Charlotte on their wedding night, but long before her birth in January 1796 they had separated acrimoniously. Princess Charlotte herself was to die in childbirth in 1817, leaving George III, despite his fifteen children, with no legitimate grandchild.

We know what Jane Austen thought of the Prince Regent. In February 1813 a letter written by Caroline to her estranged husband, listing her grievances, was published in the newspapers. "I suppose all the World is sitting in Judgement on the Princess of Wales's Letter," wrote Jane Austen. "Poor Woman, I shall support her as long as I can, because she is a Woman, & because I hate her Husband." How it must have galled her, two years later, to be obliged to dedicate her lovely *Emma* to him.

Rich and Poor

"MR RICKETTS' RETURN FROM SHOOTING" SHOWS A MIDDLE CLASS FAMILY OF THE REGENCY PERIOD.

THE SOCIETY OF THE EIGHTEENTH CENTURY was rigid and hierarchical, maintained by deference from below and paternalism from above. There was a greater degree of social mobility in Britain than in other European countries, but by and large it was influence, rather than merit that enabled a man to advance.

During Jane Austen's lifetime this rigidity was beginning to break down, as the middle classes became more numerous, more prosperous and more aspirational. The novels of her maturity demonstrate an awareness – somewhat uneasy – of these pressures from below. The assumptions of natural superiority entertained by her class were being challenged. But despite her generally conservative stance, in the young Prices, the Martins of Abbey Mill Farm, and the naval characters of *Persuasion*, she acknowledges the validity of the challenge.

The aristocracy

After the monarchy, at the top of the social pyramid came the 200 or so families whose head was a peer of the realm (Duke, Marquess, Earl, Viscount). By 1780 some had incomes touching £50,000 p.a., derived mainly from rents but often also from government office. Their country seats – of which some had more than one – were on a magnificent scale and were administered not so much as homes but as local power bases and centres of impressive hospitality. Here, and in their grand town houses, which they occupied during the parliamentary season, from January until July, they entertained, conspired, arranged dynastic marriages, dispensed political influence, and ran the country. Having no experience of life in such households – except for attending the occasional ball – Jane Austen never writes about them.

The gentry

Like the aristocracy but in a smaller way, the landed gentry also derived their incomes from rents. About a thousand of them, in Jane Austen's day, were titled, but the great majority were not. The two titled ranks were baronet, whose title passed to his eldest son, and knight, whose title died with him. Sir Thomas Bertram and Sir Walter Elliot are both baronets; Sir William Lucas and Sir Henry Russell are knights. The wives of both ranks took the title of Lady, along with their husband's surname: Lady Bertram, Lady Russell, etc. When a character in Jane Austen is known by her Christian name together with the title Lady – such as Lady Catherine de Bourgh and Lady Anne Darcy – it means her father was a peer and she retains her birthright title, whomever she marries. Lady Anne Darcy, for example, marries a commoner, albeit a rich one; her husband and son are plain Mr Darcy.

The House of Commons in Jane Austen's day was made up of the landed gentry, titled or untitled, together with the sons or other close relations of peers, and members of the Irish peerage. In the novels, both Sir Thomas Bertram and Mr Palmer (of *Sense and Sensibility*) are Members of Parliament. Others of this class were public figures locally, becoming Sheriffs of their county, Justices of the Peace and magistrates. Lady Catherine is a JP and Mr Knightley a magistrate, as was Jane's land-owning brother Edward Knight. Many others, of course, simply lived quiet private lives, without much exertion of any kind; even so, they would be looked up to as the squires of their local communities.

Sharing tastes and outlook with the landed gentry, and almost certainly intimately related to them, the minor gentry were younger sons and their families whose incomes derived chiefly from the fruits of their professions. The three professions open to gentlemen were the Church of England, the armed services and the law, in all of which Jane Austen places a number of her male characters. Together, the lesser landed gentry and the professional minor gentry constituted the world she knew and was at home in describing.

The new middle classes

Just as Jane Austen barely mentions the aristocracy, so she only glances at the existence of the members of the minor professions, whose status was at best that of "half-gentlemen" – the term is her own – used in *Emma*, that most class-conscious of novels. Surgeons and apothecaries, teachers and musicians, merchants and attorneys held a dubious place in society; they were educated men, but without "breeding" or "good connections". Beneath them were the tenant-farmers, tradesmen and clerks who constituted the lower middle class. The term middle classes, incidentally, was first used in 1797, and the term working classes in 1813. Before that the usual words for the levels of society were ranks and orders; the phrase "the lower orders" persisted into the twentieth century.

Labourers, servants and the poor

Of course the vast majority of the population lived out the whole of their miserable lives labouring or serving others. The Industrial Revolution had already begun to create the horrific living conditions of the great manufacturing towns in the Midlands and North, but this was unknown to the people of Jane Austen's world; it took the Victorians to discover what had happened in their own country. To Jane Austen, the lower orders would have meant servants, labourers on the land, and paupers, their existence accepted as part of the natural order of things. Armies of servants were employed in the great houses, while anybody with any pretensions to gentility employed at least one servant. Servants in Jane Austen's world seem well-treated and at least enjoy shelter and sufficient food. The average wage of an agricultural labourer in the period was seven or eight shillings (35-40p).

"GIN STREET" BY HOGARTH SHOWING URBAN POVERTY, THE DARK SIDE OF THE WORLD JANE AUSTEN INHABITED.

Only in *Emma* are there glimpses of the teeming poor outside the world of the great house. Emma visits a sick cottager; the ostler John Abdy cannot maintain his father who can no longer work; gypsies obtain money with menaces, and Mrs Weston's poultry houses are pilfered. Just as every other class is capable of divisions and sub-divisions, so the poor could be divided into the deserving and the undeserving. The social spectrum of Highbury, already wider than in any other Austen novel, includes both.

Church and Clergy

As THE ESTABLISHED RELIGION of the country, the Church of England held calm but powerful sway over national life. Its bishops, many of whom were related to the ruling families, sat in the House of Lords. The universities and endowed schools were under its exclusive control. Its parish churches were well-attended and its clergymen, with a few exceptions, were respected and influential in their local communities. The doctrines of the Church of England were unquestioned by all but a tiny minority. The prudent, pragmatic morality it preached, based on reason rather than revelation, and not too difficult to follow, was a significant factor in creating a quiescent and cohesive society.

"A DULL SERMON" BY JOHN COLLETT – MARY CRAWFORD WOULD ENJOY THE JOKE.

Nevertheless there were subtle changes going on in the ecclesiastical world during Jane Austen's lifetime. A century of Georgian laxity was coming to an end, to be replaced by Victorian piety that would in turn last for a hundred years. As the daughter and sister of clergymen, and as a woman to whom religion was personally important, she registered these changes with deep interest.

Incomes and patronage

The Church of England in the eighteenth century was stocked with men who looked to it for a means of livelihood rather than a vocation. It is significant that in Jane Austen's world parishes were frequently referred to as "livings", as if they only existed to provide somebody with an income for life.

Younger sons were frequently intended for the church long before their personal inclinations could be known, simply because it was a way of providing for them. Though conscientious parish priests undoubtedly existed – Mr Austen was surely one of them – it was possible for a clergyman to do very little work – or even none, if he employed a curate. Mary Crawford describes such men: "A clergyman has nothing to do but be slovenly and selfish – read the newspaper, watch the weather, and quarrel with his wife. His curate does all the work, and the business of his own life is to dine."

The standard of living enjoyed by clergymen varied enormously. Bishops could earn as much as

£7,000 p.a. At the other end of the scale were curates doing all the work of the parish in the absence of the incumbent, and earning barely more than £50 p.a. Most country parsons had a stipend of a few hundred pounds, which some were able to augment, like Mr Austen, with teaching or farming. The glebe land attached to a rectory, by enabling vegetables to be grown, was a valuable part of a clergyman's resources. Jane Austen does not often give her clergymen's incomes, but we know that the Delaford living which Colonel Brandon presents to Edward Ferrars is worth £200 p.a., while at Mansfield Parsonage Dr Grant enjoys an income of very little less than a thousand a year.

Jane Austen's own clerical brothers had widely different incomes. James eventually held three livings, amounting to £1,100. He turned down a fourth, after much heart-searching. Henry, falling back on the church for a livelihood after his bank had failed, in 1818 could get nothing better than the curacy of Chawton at £54. 12s. 0d.

Pluralism – having the care of more than one parish – which was to be frowned on later, was common in this period. So was absenteeism. In 1809, of 11,194 incumbents in England, 7,358 were non-resident. Sometimes the absentee had a private income besides his stipend and preferred to live as a gentleman of leisure. More often, inadequate stipends encouraged a parson to hold more than one benefice.

Obtaining a living was not a matter of becoming ordained and then applying to some central body for a vacancy. The cathedrals, the universities and the Crown all had livings to dispose of, but the great majority were the gift of private landowners. Some clergymen, like Edmund Bertram and Henry Tilney, know there is a family living reserved for them. Others have to attract the goodwill of a patron, as Mr Collins does of Lady Catherine, with the consequent obsequiousness that marks all his dealings with her.

Patronage, nepotism, pluralism, absenteeism, lack of independence from the landholder – taken for granted in Jane Austen's world, these were among the abuses which a new movement within the church sought to reform.

The Evangelicals

Toward the end of the eighteenth century the evangelical movement sought to bring spirituality back to a church that had become materialistic and complacent, if not corrupt. As well as a call for higher standards of personal morality, the Evangelicals encouraged Bible-reading, morning and evening family prayers, grace before meals, and Sunday observance. Personal conversion and salvation by faith were its message; enthusiastic preaching and pastoral work its methods of stirring up congregations to a more spiritual life.

At first Jane Austen, with her belief in rationality and the essentially private nature of religious feeling, was wary of such enthusiasm, which she suspected of being false or exaggerated emotion. "I do not like the Evangelicals," she stated baldly in 1809. By 1814, however, she was largely won round. Her only reservation was that people should be genuinely converted from within, not swayed by eloquent speakers: "I am by no means convinced," she wrote, "that we ought not all to be Evangelicals, & am at least persuaded that they who are so from Reason and Feeling, must be happiest & safest". In *Persuasion* Sunday travelling is a sign of Mr Elliot's moral laxity but in the earlier *Northanger Abbey* even the clergyman Henry Tilney travels on a Sunday without its seeming wrong, so much had Jane Austen's own ideas changed.

JANE'S BROTHER, THE REVEREND HENRY AUSTEN, WHO BECAME A CLERGYMAN LATE IN LIFE.

The Army

"SOLDIERS AND SAILORS are always acceptable in society. Nobody can wonder that men are soldiers and sailors," says the worldly Mary Crawford in *Mansfield Park*. She cites heroism, danger, bustle and fashion as the manly adjuncts of a military life, whether army or navy. Certainly these were the two smartest professions for men of good social standing who needed to earn a living or occupy their time until they came into their inheritance. Edward Ferrars, reviewing the professions that he might have chosen, calls the army "a great deal too smart for me" adding, "as for the navy, it had fashion on its side, but I was too old when the subject was first started to enter it."

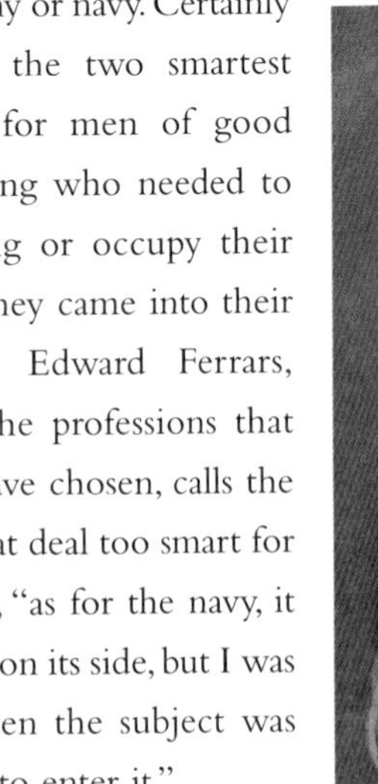

THE DUKE OF WELLINGTON IN 1812, PAINTED BY GOYA.

For this and other reasons, the army was more often the choice of the dilettante, such as Frederick Tilney, heir to Northanger Abbey, drinker and womanizer, Captain of the Twelfth Light Dragoons.

The regulars

There were two branches of the army – the regulars and the militia. The size of the regular army fluctuated according to whether peace or war prevailed. There were 110,000 regular soldiers in 1780 and 168,000 in 1800. The peace of 1802 enabled the government to court popularity by cutting back the numbers to 95,000, but as this was immediately followed by a threat of invasion the numbers were increased to 175,000. Between 1810 and 1815 they reached a new height of 300,000, but were back to a third of this within a few years of Waterloo.

The army had jobs to do even in peacetime. In the absence of a police force, it had to maintain law and order, suppressing smuggling, poaching and highway robbery and controlling riot. It also had to garrison the colonies. A body of 12,000 troops was regularly kept in Ireland.

Until 1806 enlistment was for life; after that date, shorter terms could be signed up for and men received higher rates of pay for re-enlisting. All through the period recruitment, when an upsurge in numbers was required, was by various dubious means, such as freeing criminals from prison on condition they join the army, and paying bounty to parish authorities for the impressment of their paupers. No wonder Wellington called the ordinary soldier "the scum of the earth".

This was in great contrast to the officers, who bought and sold their commissions and made legitimate if questionable profits out of equipping their regiments. Career soldiers in the novels include Colonel Brandon, who has seen service abroad, specifically the East Indies, and who returns with sufficient money to put his run-down estate in order; Colonel Fitzwilliam, younger son of an Earl with his own fortune to make; and General Tilney, the highest-ranking of any Jane Austen military character, and immensely rich, if the style of living at Northanger is any indication.

The militia

The militia was embodied only in wartime; their duties were confined to home defence, and their purpose was to free the regulars for combat abroad. Each county was under obligation to provide a quota of officers and men, who were liable for service anywhere in the country.

Because barracks were not built in England before the 1790s, soldiers were billeted in towns and became part of local society, as does Colonel Forster's regiment at Meryton, the officers dining with all the local families. In the summer it was possible to camp out, as this particular regiment does at Brighton. George Wickham admits "it was the prospect of constant society, and good society," which was his chief inducement to join the militia. When disgraced and forced to flee his debts, he is nevertheless able, with Mr Darcy's financial assistance, to embark on a new career in the regulars.

Twenty-five years before the action of *Emma*, Mr Weston "had satisfied an active cheerful mind and social temper by entering into the militia of his county, then embodied". It is the social and geographical chances of his military life that introduce him to Miss Churchill, of a great Yorkshire family, a lady whom he would not otherwise have met.

Jane Austen's brother Henry also looked to the militia to get on in life. He joined the militia not of his own county but of Oxfordshire, as a lieutenant, in 1793 when Britain declared war on France. The life of a soldier suited him, though perhaps out of deference to his parents, he had not completely given up all thoughts of a clerical career. However, in January 1796, he was, according to Jane, "hankering after the Regulars" and "has got a scheme in his head about getting a lieutenancy and adjutancy in the 86th, a new-raised regiment, which he fancies will be ordered to the Cape of Good Hope." This came to nothing, but by the following year he had gained promotion within the militia. Eliza, about to accept his offer of marriage at last, described him as:

> *Captain, Paymaster & Adjutant. He is a very lucky young man & bids fair to possess a considerable share of riches & honours. I believe he has now given up all thoughts of the Church, & he is right for he certainly is not so fit for a parson as a soldier.*

Henry's military career secured him not only the wife of his choice, but acquaintances who would be useful to him in his later business life. By 1801 he had left the militia and was living in London, where he set up with two former fellow-officers as a firm of bankers, which prospered until the post-Waterloo crash of 1816.

TYPICAL RECRUITING METHODS IN THE EIGHTEENTH CENTURY.

The Royal Navy

LORD NELSON'S FUNERAL PROCESSION ON THE THAMES FROM GREENWICH TO WHITEHALL IN 1806.

DURING JANE AUSTEN'S LIFETIME, the Royal navy was held in increasingly high regard by the country, as its crucial role in frustrating French attempts at world domination was appreciated. The Battle of Trafalgar of 1805, which Francis Austen narrowly missed, to his very great chagrin, was perhaps the first sea battle whose name inspired the same patriotic pride in the public consciousness as the land battles of Agincourt, Blenheim and so forth had traditionally done.

The cult of Admiral Nelson, whose death at Trafalgar was followed by a spate of biographies – "I am sick of Lives of Nelson," Jane Austen once wrote – and the lasting memorial of Trafalgar Square and Nelson's Column, were evidence of public triumphalism in the naval supremacy that Britain was to enjoy without dispute for a century from 1805. Jane Austen, with two beloved brothers in the navy, certainly shared this naval fervour, losing no opportunity to honour the profession in her last completed novel, *Persuasion*.

Conditions in the navy

"I do assure you," says Mrs Croft, who has accompanied her husband to sea in five different ships, "that nothing can exceed the accommodations of a man of war." Her brother Captain Wentworth also ridicules the company for "supposing sailors to be living on board without anything to eat, or any cook to dress it if there were, or any servant to wait, or any knife and fork to use".

Despite these eulogies life at sea was harsh, dreadfully so for the ordinary seaman. Flogging was commonplace. Diet consisted of salt beef or pork, hard cheese, unleavened bread or biscuit and a gallon of beer per day. Not only was this fatally lacking in Vitamin C, it was hard and indigestible. The efficacy of fresh fruit, especially citrus fruit, and green vegetables in helping men to recover from scurvy had been noticed as early as the middle of the eighteenth century, but it was not until 1795 that naval personnel were issued with daily juice of lemons or limes.

Particularly susceptible to scurvy were the pressed men captured for royal naval service on their way into home ports from a long voyage on a merchantman. Although the notorious press gangs did operate on land, rounding up men in ports, the majority of men were obtained afloat, the best source of experienced seamen. During the French Revolutionary and Napoleonic Wars, the ratio of volunteers to pressed men varied from 50:50 at the beginning of the period to 25:75 toward the end. And many of those recorded as volunteers were really pressed men, who chose to take the bounty (between £1 and £3) when they realized they stood no chance of escape.

During the same war, of the approximately 100,000 naval personnel who lost their lives, only 7 per cent was by enemy action, while 13 per cent was by shipwreck, 20 per cent by accident and 60 per cent by disease. In addition to scurvy, typhus, which was spread by lice among men living at close quarters, was a major killer on board.

Ships and men

Warships were divided into ships of the line, carrying from 60 to 100 guns, and cruisers – frigates, sloops and brigs with fewer guns. In 1810 British naval strength was 152 ships of the line and 390 cruisers. There were 800 captains, 600 commanders and 3,270 lieutenants on active service, in command of 142,000 seamen, of whom 30,000 were marines. The marines were a special category of fighting men, trained in small arms to fight in naval battles and beach assaults, but not expected to be proficient in seamanship. Mr Price is an officer in the marines, and in marrying him Miss Frances Ward thoroughly "disobliges" her family.

The careers of Jane Austen's two sailor brothers illustrate the difficulties and rewards of being an officer in the navy. They both began their careers at the Royal Naval Academy, Portsmouth at the age of twelve, and first went to sea at fifteen. It was thought desirable for boys to start at sea young, to accustom them to the hard life they could expect.

Boys would attach themselves to a captain – a relation or family friend – and hope, by gaining his good opinion, to secure his help in looking for promotion. In return he gained the loyalty and effort of his junior officers. Unlike in the army, naval commissions could not be bought. Patronage was essential in the early stages of a young man's career, when knowing someone influential hastened promotion, as Jane's anxious letters about her brothers, and the episode concerning William Price and Admiral Crawford in *Mansfield Park* make clear.

Prize money was the way that naval officers could hope to get rich, in war time at least. The captain would receive one quarter the value of a captured ship, the other ranks taking smaller proportions, and the ordinary seamen dividing the final quarter between them all. The arrangement did give even pressed men some incentive to practise good seamanship and fight well. Young Charles Austen spent his first £30 prize money on topaz crosses for his sisters; the prize money gained by Francis Austen for his part in the battle of Santo Domingo enabled him to marry; in *Persuasion*, Captain Wentworth has realized £20,000 in eight years' warfare. Unlike today, he and his brother officers actually looked forward to another war, as did Jane Austen's brothers, both of whom eventually rose to the rank of Admiral, displaying diligence, good judgement and fearless leadership at every stage of their careers.

CHARLES AUSTEN, JANE AUSTEN'S YOUNGER SAILOR BROTHER, AT THE TIME OF HIS WEDDING.

Revolution and War

FOR ALMOST ALL OF JANE AUSTEN'S adult life, Great Britain was at war with France. She was seventeen when the war began in 1793, and nearly forty when it ended for good in 1815 with the battle of Waterloo. She and her generation lived with the constant possibility, if not the constant threat, of invasion or blockade. Her brothers' active service in the Royal Navy meant that she was more aware of the dangers than most.

REPUBLICAN POSTER OF 1793.

Jane Austen's dislike of France, and her horror of social disorder, were bound up together, and probably had their roots in the same event. She was eighteen when, on 22 February 1794, her cousin Eliza's husband, the Comte de Feuillide, was guillotined in Paris. The charge against him was that he had bribed an official not to prosecute a friend, an elderly widow, for planting her fields with fodder crops with the intention of producing famine in the country.

THE EXECUTION OF LOUIS XIV – HE AND HIS QUEEN, MARIE ANTOINETTE, WERE GUILLOTINED IN 1793.

The French Revolution

In 1789, France was in a pitiful state. A succession of costly and unsuccessful wars had left the Treasury bankrupt, and at a loss to know where to look for new taxes. The harvest of the previous two years had failed, so many poor people were starving. The gulf between the ostentation of the court and aristocracy, and the poverty of the ordinary people, was much greater even than in England. An increasing number of the educated middle classes, influenced by the political writings of Rousseau and Voltaire, were beginning to demand a democratically elected government for France. In May King Louis XVI called the first States-General, or Assembly, for 175 years. His concessions were too little and too late. On 14 July, the Paris mob stormed the Bastille, a state prison regarded as a symbol of the King's tyrannical rule. In October they captured the King and his Queen, Marie Antoinette, at Versailles.

Over the next two years extremists gained control of the Assembly and the reign of Terror escalated, with thousands of people, including eventually the King and Queen, sent to the guillotine. The Revolution was out of control, and people across the Channel looked on with conflicting emotions.

The British response

"Bliss was it in that dawn to be alive / But to be young was very heaven," wrote Wordsworth at the beginning of the Revolution, when the ideals of liberty and equality seemed about to be realized for the first time in any western society. For quite different reasons Britain's Prime Minister Pitt also welcomed the French Revolution, believing that internal turmoil would deflect France from her old ambition of dominating Europe. As late as 1792, Pitt declared that Europe could look forward to at least fifteen years of peace.

The MP Edmund Burke, on the other hand, in 1790 prophesied the emergence of a French dictator and a long war. The British public recoiled from the massacres going on in France – even

WELLINGTON AND THE PRUSSIAN COMMANDER BLÜCHER WERE VICTORIOUS AT THE BATTLE OF WATERLOO.

Wordsworth revised his opinions – and those with a vested interest in the social order became seriously frightened that revolutionary ideas would spread to Britain. This was especially the case after November 1792, when the French issued the Edict of Fraternity, inciting the lower orders everywhere to join the Revolution. When added to the virulent expansionism that revolutionary France began to display, the British government felt it could no longer stand by, and war was declared.

The fluctuations of war

The first nine years of the war were waged with revolutionary France, and were inconclusive. Britain gained naval supremacy in the Mediterranean, but France, under the military leadership of the brilliant young Napoleon Bonaparte, remained undefeated and dominant on the Continent.

By 1802 both sides were exhausted and ready for peace. From the British point of view, the worst excesses of the Revolution were over, and Napoleon seemed to be establishing a stable government in France. "A peace which all men are glad of, but no man could be proud of," in Sheridan's words, the Peace of Amiens was signed in 1802. It lasted just fourteen months. Napoleon, who was about to declare himself Emperor of France, had not really given up his dream of conquest. The next twelve years of conflict were to be known as the Napoleonic Wars.

In the summer of 1804 Napoleon gathered a large fleet for invasion of Britain. The threat was a serious one, but the Royal Navy foiled his plans in a series of chases, which ended in the victory of Trafalgar in October 1805.

Napoleon's next ploy, from 1806 to 1812, was the Continental System, whereby he attempted to deny Britain her markets and seriously weaken her economy. It was only partially effective, however, and Napoleon also met with reverses when the land war moved to the Spanish peninsula, where Wellington proved himself the most effective military leader Britain had known for a century.

Napoleon next made the mistake of looking for conquest to the east. The advance on Moscow of 1812 was a disaster for him, wiping out a large part of his army in the terrible winter conditions. For the first time, four great powers – Russia, Prussia, Austria and Britain – were united against him. They invaded France and occupied Paris in March 1814. Napoleon abdicated, and was allowed to retire to the island of Elba in the Mediterranean, from where ten months later he escaped to France, but his "Hundred Days" of renewed power was ended by the Battle of Waterloo on 18 June 1815. This time he was exiled to St Helena in the South Atlantic where he died in 1821.

The British Empire

DURING THE GEORGIAN and Regency periods, Britain was acquiring and maintaining its colonies partly for prestige but mainly for commercial advantage. The ever-growing population of the colonies provided Britain with markets for her manufactured goods, while raw materials, especially from her tropical possessions, could be cheaply imported, processed and re-exported. In return for these benefits, the colonies could look for military protection from the imperial power.

Colonial trade was the engine for both the industrial revolution and the naval supremacy that were to make the country so invincible in the next century. At the same time, large-scale commitments abroad carried the seeds of their own eventual destruction. Jane Austen's lifetime coincided with the beginning of this cycle.

WARREN HASTINGS ON HIS ELEPHANT.

India and Warren Hastings

In the early part of the eighteenth century the English East India Company had three settlements, Bombay, Madras and Bengal, through which it sent cotton, silk, ivory and spices to Britain. It was a private company whose only interest was a mercantile one. By the 1770s the increasing administrative burden resulted in Warren Hastings being appointed as the first Governor-General. He established a civil service and mechanisms for justice and tax collection over a vast terrain. He also defended the territory of the Company from France, who sent expeditions and tried to incite the Indian princes against the British.

But when Hastings returned to England in 1785 it was to face impeachment on charges of corruption. The trial in the House of Lords dragged on from 1788 to 1795, a public spectacle for visitors to London. He was acquitted on every count. Although bankrupted by the expense of the trial, he received a generous pension from the Company for the rest of his life.

The Austen family had various links with Warren Hastings. As young men Hastings and George Austen had known one another in Kent. When Hastings wanted to send his infant son back to England, it was to George Austen he entrusted him. In fact the boy died while under the Austens' care, and Mrs Austen is said to have mourned him as if he had been a son of her own. When Hastings also lost his wife, he appears to have turned for comfort to George's sister Philadelphia, then married and living in India. Her daughter Eliza, Jane Austen's cousin, was almost certainly the offspring of this illicit union. The Austens kept up their friendship with Hastings after his return to Britain. Henry Austen, by then Eliza's husband, wrote to congratulate him on his acquittal. When *Pride and Prejudice* was published, Henry sent him a copy and passed on his response to the author. "I am quite delighted with what such a Man writes about it," Jane reported.

In the years following Hastings' departure, expansion of British power on the sub-continent continued almost against the will of the government who accepted the added responsibilities and costs with some reluctance. Only later would India come to be regarded as the Jewel in the Crown of the British Empire.

The West Indies

Britain's West Indian possessions included the Bermudas, Bahamas, Jamaica, the Virgin Islands, St Kitts, Antigua, Montserrat and Barbados. In terms of trade, they were the most valuable of British colonies

SLAVES CUTTING SUGAR CANE ON ANTIGUA, WHERE SIR THOMAS BERTRAM OWNED A PLANTATION.

at this time. They needed negro slaves for their plantations, captured and shipped from Africa by British merchants. They supplied Britain with sugar, and took British textiles for the slaves to wear and luxury goods for the white population.

The island of Antigua is the source of much of Sir Thomas Bertram's wealth in *Mansfield Park*. Because these revenues really matter to him – to the extent of causing him to spend two years away from home – it can be deduced that his estate in England is not sufficient to support the style of life he aspires to.

Various members of the Austen family derived their income directly from the West Indies. Mrs Austen's brother James Leigh Perrot married Jane Cholmeley, heiress to an estate in Barbados. Mr Austen's friend James Nibbs, whose portrait hung at Steventon Rectory and who was godfather to the eldest son, James, owned plantations on Antigua and made George Austen a trustee of his property. James Austen's first wife Anne Mathew, mother of Anna Lefroy, was the daughter of General Mathew, Commander-in-Chief of the Windward and Leeward Islands and Governor of Grenada. Charles Austen married the daughter of the former Attorney General of Bermuda, whom he met while on duty there. A relation of Mr Austen's on his mother's side, Sir George Hampson, had property in Jamaica, and two of Mr Austen's nephews, William and George Walter, went out to work for him there. So many instances within one family indicate the extent to which the colonies enriched the middle and upper classes of Britain.

France was Britain's competitor for these riches. In the clashes between the great powers over their colonies, young men might meet either glory or death. Cassandra's fiancée, Tom Fowle, army chaplain to Lord Craven's regiment, died of yellow fever (a virulent form of malaria) off Santo Domingo, one of 80,000 British men to submit to tropical disease during a five year campaign against the French in the Caribbean. Tom had been hoping to make enough money to marry; eight years later, Francis Austen successfully realized the same hopes when he shared in the glory and prize money of the 1806 naval battle of Santo Domingo.

The New World

"A STRANGE BUSINESS this in America, Dr Grant! – What is your opinion?" says Tom Bertram, who has just been reading the newspaper, and who has to find some topic of conversation quickly. We will never know what the strange business is, but Britain was at war with the United States during most of the writing of *Mansfield Park*.

NEW YORK CITY AT THE TIME OF INDEPENDENCE.

Fiercely patriotic, Jane Austen shared with many people of her time and class the view that Americans must be uncivilized, even heathen. During the 1812–14 war she was staying with her brother Henry in London, and wrote, for her, at unusual length on the subject of foreign affairs:

> *His view, & the view of those he mixes with, of Politics, is not chearful [sic] – with regard to an American war I mean; – they consider it as certain, & what is to ruin us. The Americans cannot be conquered, & we shall only be teaching them the skill in War which they may now want. We are to make them good Sailors & Soldiers, & gain nothing ourselves.– If we are to be ruined, it cannot be helped – but I place my hope of better things on a claim to the protection of Heaven, as a Religious Nation, a Nation in spite of much Evil improving in Religion which I cannot believe the Americans to possess.*

The loss of the United States

The thirteen eastern seaboard territories of the North American continent had been founded not by government-controlled expeditions but by private trading companies or religious refugees. Separated from Great Britain by three thousand miles of Atlantic Ocean across which it took an average of seven weeks to sail, the colonies were accustomed to running their own affairs, though each had a Governor appointed by the Crown. In the early part of the century, the Governor of South Carolina was Lord Craven, whose great-grand-daughter Caroline Mary Craven Austen, named after him by her rather snobbish mother, was Jane Austen's niece.

By the 1770s, the British were looking for a greater share of the burden of colonial administration to be placed on the settlers, while on the other side the settlers' famous cry was "no taxation without representation". The first clash of arms came in 1775, the year of Jane Austen's birth. France and Spain joined the war on the side of the colonists. It was a war which Britain, badly led, hampered by long distances and already engaged in conflict in other parts of the world, could not win. The war was concluded by the Treaty of Versailles in 1783, recognizing the independence of the United States of America.

The loss of the American colonies was more significant in terms of prestige than in economic interests. After the war, trade between the two countries continued to expand, despite prejudice against it on both sides. British exports to America rose from three million pounds in 1793 to seven million in 1800.

The 1812–1814 war

After the lapse of nearly thirty years a second war broke out, one with much less to win or lose on either side. In 1812 the United States government declared war on a Britain that was in the thick of its long-running struggle with France. For several years the Americans had understandably been growing annoyed at British action in stopping and searching neutral shipping. Among the naval officers engaged in this duty was Jane's brother Charles Austen, who spent nearly seven years away from home on the North American station.

Conflict between Britain and her former colony took place mostly at sea and along the Canadian border. While British ships raided ports along the American coast, some US ships crossed the Atlantic and attacked British shipping in the English Channel. After a US army had invaded Canada and set fire to York, now Toronto, the British retaliated by burning buildings in Washington, including the home of the President, James Madison. It is said that he fled so swiftly British officers were able to sit down to a dinner his servants had cooked for him. To hide the marks of the flames this house was whitewashed, and so became known as the White House. In December 1814 the Treaty of Ghent was signed, bringing this particularly futile war to an end.

Canada

Canada had been acquired from the French in 1763 and after the American War of Independence many people had chosen to leave the American colonies to live in Canada under the British flag. They were known as Empire Loyalists. In 1791, Pitt's Canada Constitutional Act divided the country into two provinces: Upper Canada (English-speaking Ontario) and Lower Canada (French-speaking Quebec).

GEORGE WASHINGTON (1732–1799), FIRST PRESIDENT OF THE UNITED STATES.

During the war of 1812–14, both provinces united in repulsing American invasion. But there continued to be resentment by the Catholic French population of Canada that an English-speaking Protestant Governor had jurisdiction over their affairs. As part of the Treaty of Ghent, four boundary commissions were set up to examine the frontier between the USA and Canada, although this was not settled for good until 1846.

Slave trade & Transportation

SLAVES IN THE HOLD OF A SHIP TRANSPORTING THEM ACROSS THE ATLANTIC.

BRITISH SHIPS WERE PLYING the oceans of the world during the greater part of Jane Austen's life, engaged in traffic of two shameful kinds. One was the transportation of convicted criminals from the home country to the Australian continent. The other was the shipment of African people from ports along the eastern seaboard of Africa to the southern states of America and the Caribbean islands of the West Indies, where they were sold into slavery.

In both instances, the miserable conditions on board ship, and the inhumane purpose of the traffic, were in stark contrast to the leisured and elegant lives of the British gentry of the time, most of whom, if they thought about such unpleasant topics at all, accepted what was being done in their name as part of the natural order of things.

Transportation and Aunt Leigh Perrot

In a series of voyages at about the time of Jane Austen's birth, Captain Cook was exploring and taking possession of that part of the Australian continent he named New South Wales. But it was only when the loss of the American colonies forced the British government to look for a new place to send convicts that they became at all interested in this vast, far-away land. The first batch of convicts were landed at Sydney in 1788. Other convict settlements were made at Hobart, Brisbane and Melbourne in the next twenty years.

Jane Austen's aunt, the rich and respectable Mrs Jane Leigh Perrot, came very close to being transported to Australia when in 1799 she was accused of stealing some lace from a shop in Bath. The lace was valued at one shilling (5p), and her arrest may have been an attempt at blackmail, for it seems most likely that the lace was planted on her. It was wrapped up, surely by the shop-owner, in a parcel of other goods she had paid for. Mrs Leigh Perrot, who was a strong-minded woman, decided to stand trial and proclaim her innocence rather than submit to blackmail. She was taking a great risk. In theory the death penalty could be imposed for any crime of larceny, however small, but in practice convicted thieves were usually transported.

Mrs Leigh Perrot was remanded in custody in disgusting conditions at Ilchester Jail in Somerset between August 1799 and March 1800, when her trial was held at the Spring Assizes. Mrs Austen offered one or both of her daughters as support to their aunt at the trial, an experience that would have been for Jane Austen, then aged twenty-four, quite unlike anything else in her life. Her aunt generously did not take up the offer, saying that to have her nieces looked at in a public court would be too painful.

After a trial lasting seven hours, Mrs Leigh Perrot was acquitted of the charge, but such a result was by no means inevitable. Her devoted husband had made contingency plans to sell his property in England and accompany his wife to Australia, where the way of life would have been unimaginably different from that they were used to in elegant Bath.

JANE AUSTEN'S AUNT LEIGH PERROT.

The slave trade

Until people began to have a conscience about it, the slave trade was a very lucrative business for Britain. Ships would leave British ports, especially Bristol, laden with trinkets for Africa. Having bribed some of the natives to round up their fellow countrymen – including and women and children – these would then be taken on board in dreadful conditions for the long voyage to America and the West Indies, where they were sold as slaves. The third leg of the voyage was the return to England with sugar, cotton and other raw commodities from the New World.

At the height of the trade, 74,000 slaves were being exported each year from Africa to America, 38,000 of them in British ships. William Wilberforce was the leading figure in the movement to abolish the slave trade on religious and humanitarian grounds. In 1807 an Act was passed forbidding the participation of British subjects in the slave trade and the importation of slaves into British colonies.

In *Emma*, Mrs Elton is quick to protest that her brother-in-law Mr Suckling – a resident of Bristol – always favoured the abolition. In *Mansfield Park*, on Sir Thomas Bertram's return from Antigua, Fanny shyly asks him about the slave trade. The silence of the other members of the family, who are completely uninterested in the island which guarantees them their comfortable lifestyle, prevents her continuing her enquiries. She might be asking Sir Thomas how the island is faring now that there is no fresh supply of labour. Or she might be asking him whether the abolition really has been effective. There was, after all, no way of enforcing it except by ships of the British navy stopping and searching suspect vessels. It took some years for the trade to dry up altogether, and many more before the slaves already on the plantations were set free.

WILLIAM WILBERFORCE, CAMPAIGNER AGAINST THE SLAVE TRADE.

Farming

THE WORLD JANE AUSTEN knew was based on the ownership of land. Status was conferred by it, lifestyle guaranteed by it. Through enclosure, through purchase and through marriage, large estates were accumulated in the hands of the few. By the end of the eighteenth century, nearly half the cultivated land of Britain was held by just five thousand families.

Land was valued not so much for profitable investment as for the prestige and political power that it brought. Possession of land was the entrée to county society and to participation in local affairs. All the civil and military administration in the provinces was managed by the Lords-Lieutenant, Sheriffs and Justices of the Peace who were drawn from landed society. National politics, too, were in the hands of the great landholders, as was patronage of the church and armed services, so that younger sons and other connections could be helped to get on, consolidating the wealth of the entire family.

MR KNIGHTLEY, GENTLEMAN FARMER, WITH AGRICULTURAL LABOURERS IN THE BACKGROUND.

"New" money from business enterprise almost always found its way into land. A case in point is Samuel Whitbread, founder of the London brewing firm. Having acquired 12,000 acres of good farming land in the Home Counties, he bought himself into Parliament, where he was followed by his son. By the mid-1790s the Whitbread farms were bringing in £12,000 p.a., but this still did not equal the profits being made from beer.

There was a fruitful cross-fertilization, in fact, between business and land ownership in Britain. Landholders were more open than their European counterparts to exploiting their land in such enterprises as mining or the construction of canals. This swelled the income from agricultural rents, which doubled between 1790 and 1810. The food requirements of a growing population, many of them newly living in towns, raised prices and provided a powerful incentive to increase yields by ingenious new methods.

Agricultural reform

Large farms were more economic. The old system of cultivation by strips in open fields worked by the whole village, with everyone having rights to common and waste land, was fast disappearing. Enclosure into the kind of fields we know today, bordered by hedges and in private ownership, had been taking place for a century or more, but the new incentives meant the process was now completed. By 1800, it was estimated that only half a dozen counties remained in the whole of England with more than three per cent of their land unenclosed.

The appearance of the countryside was transformed into the lovely patchwork that now seems so typically and immemorially English. The other effect of enclosure was that a whole class of peasant proprietors was extinguished, forced either into becoming hired agricultural labourers, or turning to the towns for new types of employment. The land was not denuded, for the population everywhere was increasing. But within forty years of Jane Austen's death, there would be fewer people engaged in agriculture than in other occupations for the first time in Britain's history.

Other agricultural reforms of this period included crop rotation, so that no field need lie fallow, and the cultivation of turnips, which meant cattle could be kept alive through the winter. The art of stock breeding was refined. Jethro Tull invented the seed-drill, which sowed seed in rows by a horse-drawn device, replacing the time-honoured method of broadcasting by hand. The invention of the threshing machine in 1788 was followed by a chaff-cutting machine to produce cattle fodder. Most farmers and landholders were slow to adopt new ways. In 1793, at the outbreak of the war with France, the government were sufficiently concerned about food supplies to establish a Board of Agriculture, by means of which these innovations, and others which followed, could be disseminated.

The success of Britain's farming community in meeting the new challenges is measured by the fact that by 1800 wool and mutton output had doubled compared with a century earlier, and grain production had kept pace with a population increase of some seventy per cent.

DECORATION FROM A MAP IN HENRY HOBDEN'S "ATLAS OF KNIGHT FAMILY ESTATES".

Jane Austen and the land

Growing up in a family that included farming among its activities gave Jane Austen a deep appreciation of the land. She shared the sentiments expressed by Cassandra in a letter to a cousin: "I quite envy you your Farm, there is so much amusement and so many comforts attending a Farm in the country that those who have once felt the advantages cannot easily forget them". Jane exchanged informed remarks about the weather and the harvest with neighbours, and she gave her interest in the subject to Fanny Price, who travelling through an unknown stretch of country, finds entertainment "in observing the appearance of the country, the bearings of the roads, the difference of soil, the state of the harvest, the cottages, the cattle, the children". But just as *Mansfield Park* is Jane Austen's clerical novel; and *Persuasion* her celebration of the naval profession, so *Emma* is her farming novel. The hero, Mr Knightley, is a gentleman farmer, deeply involved in his land "Why should he marry?" as Emma herself once asks. "He is as happy as possible by himself; with his farm, and his sheep, and his library, and all the parish to manage." His relations with William Larkin, his farm bailiff, and Robert Martin, the tenant farmer, are exemplary. Robert Martin is a new kind of man for a Jane Austen novel, she is not quite comfortable in his society – not comfortable enough to report his direct speech. But she shares Mr Knightley's estimation of him, and knows that it is this new type of farmer, better educated than his forbears, taking an intelligent interest in his work (he reads the Agricultural Reports) and rising in prosperity, who will produce the food needed to sustain the community even in the face of war.

FARMING ACTIVITIES C. 1800.

An Industrial Nation

To say the Industrial Revolution brought about the most profound and thoroughgoing change experienced by any society in the history of civilization is not to exaggerate. That it began about the time of Jane Austen's childhood, in the small off-shore island in which she happened to have been born, is one of those interesting conjunctions of history, which may seem wholly random and without significance. She did not, after all, witness much of the urbanization and industrialization of Britain, or explore these issues in her novels. What were known as "Condition of England" novels did not appear until the 1840s, twenty or thirty years after her death, when the results – for good or bad – of these unplanned and unregulated processes began to impinge on the consciousness of the educated classes. Had she lived as long as her sister and brothers, the last of whom died in 1865, she may well have contributed to this debate, for she was certainly always deeply interested in the condition of England as she perceived it.

But the fact that her formative years coincided with the onset of the Industrial Revolution may not be quite as accidental as first appears. The conditions that favoured human ingenuity and enterprise, allowed freedom of thought and where the arts and sciences both flourished, were also those which stimulated a young woman in a country rectory to write her serious but amusing novels.

The Industrial Revolution

Many of the pre-conditions which combined to produce this unique revolution have been touched on already. The new agricultural efficiency supported an

BEDLAM FURNACE IN SHROPSHIRE, CRADLE OF THE INDUSTRIAL REVOLUTION, 1803.

ever-increasing population who, freed from the necessity to work the land, were available for new kinds of work in factories, mills, mines and towns. As a commercial nation, Britain had seen a steadily rising standard of living, creating demand for luxury consumer goods and new inventions. Her maritime empire created vast new markets and provided a cheap supply of raw commodities. Geographical factors included a large indented coastline with many good ports, fast-flowing streams for water-power, an equable climate – dampness is ideal for the manufacture of cotton – and good reserves of coal and other mineral resources.

Iron, coal and steam

The inventions and developments themselves were highly interdependent. Iron had traditionally been refined from ore using charcoal in small woodland clearances. New methods of smelting with coke in blast-furnaces enabled much greater quantities of iron to be produced, essential for all the other processes that followed. By 1797 Britain was able to produce more iron than she needed and to export the surplus. Better quality iron, suitable for wrought ironwork, was made possible by the invention of the puddling process by Henry Cort, a naval contractor and iron-master of Fontley in Hampshire. This more malleable iron, better at taking stresses and strains, was essential for industrial purposes; but it also made possible the exquisite wrought ironwork of the Regency resorts like Cheltenham, known to Jane Austen, where balconies and railings impart delicacy to the street scene.

Britain had long had a small coal-mining industry, but a combination of increased demand and technical innovation meant that production more than doubled in the second half of the eighteenth century to ten million tons in 1800. The first use of the steam engine as a source of power was developed to pump water from mines. Its potential was soon realized. In 1781 James Watt fitted a crank-shaft and cogwheel to the piston, which gave it a rotary movement, capable of turning machinery and therefore of powering innumerable industrial processes in the new factories which sprang up all over the north of Britain. Living as she did in the south of England, these developments were hardly visible to Jane Austen. But one aspect of the Industrial Revolution did touch her closely, in a very literal sense.

CHILD WORKERS AT A LANCASHIRE COTTON MILL.

King Cotton

Jane Austen and her contemporaries and characters were largely clothed in cotton from the new Lancastrian mills. The fabric was valued for its cheapness, washability and comfort in wear, and could be adapted either for high fashion or for affordable clothing for the masses at home and abroad. Successive inventions by Kay, Hargreaves, Crompton, Cartwright and others had transformed a hand-craft carried out in the homes of spinners and weavers to a fully mechanized industry. In 1801, imports of raw cotton amounted to 56,000,000 lb., while the value of exported cotton goods was £7,050,000.

The first mills relied upon water-power and were built by the side of fast-flowing Pennine streams, but from the 1780s steam-power was introduced to the industry and factories could be built in towns. While there were only two cotton mills in Manchester in 1782, ten years later there were fifty-two, each employing about 300 workers.

Cotton was perhaps the single most important of the new industries, bringing enormous wealth to individual mill-owners and to the nation – and untold misery, let it be said, to the operatives. Many of these were women and children, as they were more docile, accepted lower pay, and had more nimble fingers for the thread. Their long hours and inhumane working conditions were to provide factory reformers with their first cause, but this was some time after Jane Austen's death.

Whigs, Conservatives and Radicals

CARTOON OF 1796, WILLIAM PITT CRUSHING THE OPPOSITION TO CONTINUE THE WAR.

THE PERIOD 1788 TO 1812, covering most of Jane Austen's adult life, saw a significant realignment in politics. The various pressures of revolution, war, madness and regency brought about a splintering of the old Whig party and the creation of a new Conservative party – though not as yet so-named. Outside Parliament, the period also witnessed the first stirrings of political consciousness on the part of the disenfranchised in the Radical movement. After 1812, a measure of stability returned to the political scene, though its inherent weaknesses were to find vent twenty years later in the great Reform Act.

Background to political life

The basis of politics in the late eighteenth century was still the struggle between Parliament and the Sovereign, which George III, by asserting his rights, had renewed after the lethargy of the first two Georges. The Act of Settlement had left the monarch with the power of choosing ministers and thus, by extension, policies. In theory he also had the power to veto parliamentary legislation, though shrewd awareness of the possible consequences of such abuse meant that in fact he never did.

The two-party system existed in embryo, but there were many more independent members, more short-lived factions and splinter-groups, more changing party allegiance from policy to policy than today, and certainly no use of the whip. Given this fluidity, in broad terms the Whigs traditionally represented the aristocracy and the Tories the interest of the landed gentry, the class to which the Austens belonged. There was, of course, nobody to represent the interests of people without land at all. Since the King favoured Tory policies to keep the otherwise powerful Whigs in check, this more or less balanced out.

Another effective balance was that between the Commons and the Lords. Though most offices of state were held by peers who sat in the House of Lords, the all-important control over finance and taxation was vested in the House of Commons. Chancellors of the Exchequer had to be appointed from among commoners. Constituencies bore no relation to patterns of population. The county of Cornwall sent 44 members to Westminster, while the new cities of Birmingham, Leeds, Manchester and Sheffield were unrepresented. Voting qualifications varied enormously from borough to borough, but no place came anywhere near democratic ideals. In 77 seats the electorate numbered fewer than one hundred; very often elections were uncontested. In 1780 fewer than one Englishman in eight could vote, the proportion becoming even lower as the population grew; and of course, no woman had the vote.

Pitt and Fox

For much of Jane Austen's life the Prime Minister was William Pitt the Younger. As the nearest thing to a Tory (his followers owned no name but Pittites) he would have commanded the general support of the Austens, just as he did, by and large, of the King. He was Prime Minister from 1783 to 1801, and again from 1804 to his death in 1806.

The opposition party, the Whigs, had lost their dominance of earlier in the century since the accession of George III. Led by Charles James Fox, the Whigs had the nominal support of the Prince of Wales, according to the time-honoured Hanoverian tradition whereby the heir to the throne always took the opposite party line from the Sovereign. But Prinny's frivolous support proved to be hardly worth having.

The weakness of Fox's leadership was displayed in the constitutional crisis of the King's first bout of madness in 1788. His recovery the next year was a stroke of luck for Pitt, for the Regent would certainly have had him out. Almost immediately there followed the French Revolution which, although welcomed at first as we have seen, as it moved towards regicide and terror soon began to infect the British political classes with fear. A coalition concerned to conserve property and the old order at all costs was struck between Pittites and those Whigs who were more frightened of internal sedition than of anything else.

Meanwhile the Foxites held that the true Whig creed lay in defence of the liberties of Englishmen and the promotion of mild reform. In this they were motivated not, as may be supposed, by concern for the disadvantaged, but by anxiety to limit the powers of the Crown. They were the most aristocratic group in Parliament, and their thought processes remained wedded to the old eighteenth century polarities.

Following Pitt's death in January 1806 there was a so-called "Ministry of all the Talents" in which Fox served as Foreign Secretary, his first office for twenty-three years; but he too died in September that year, and the Ministry itself fell next March. With the death of these two great Parliamentary figures, politics lost some of its bite. There were five weak governments between 1801 and 1812, ending in the assassination of Spencer Percival – the only British Prime Minister to be killed in office – in 1812.

The Rights of Man

The 1790s witnessed the first national political movement for 150 years which involved the lower orders to a significant degree. The Radical call for reform was taken up by Tom Paine in his book *The Rights of Man*, published cheaply in two parts in 1791 and 92. Paine's targets were unearned privilege and inherited wealth; he called for universal male franchise, deplored all wars, and advocated spending the money thus saved upon very twentieth-century concepts, old-age pensions, family allowances and free education for all. The propertied classes were horrified. By 1795 Radicalism had been driven underground by a tranche of repressive measures introduced by Pitt. It would emerge again, but not until after Jane Austen's life.

CHARLES JAMES FOX, LEADER OF THE WHIGS.

Poetry

WATERCOLOUR AND INK ILLUSTRATION FOR "JERUSALEM" BY WILLIAM BLAKE.

In Persuasion, when Anne Elliot and Captain Benwick fall into a discussion of poetry, they agree upon one thing: "the richness of the present age". Jane Austen and her characters show familiarity with the poetry of their times. The list of poets mentioned or alluded to in her letters and novels include, from her childhood or earlier, Pope, Gray, Thomson and Cowper; and among her contemporaries, Burns, Scott, Byron, Crabbe, Wordsworth and Southey. She mentions other minor poets but neglects to mention two other great names publishing during her lifetime, Blake and Coleridge.

Though the brightest stars among this myriad are those we think of as the Romantic poets of the post-Revolutionary era, Jane Austen's deep attachment to the culture of the eighteenth century is nowhere more apparent than in her poetic preferences.

Cowper

We know, because both her brother and her nephew tell us in their recollections of Jane Austen, that her favourite poet was William Cowper. Cowper, who was born in 1731 and died in 1800, was an exact contemporary of Jane Austen's father. His poetry was written and published in the 1780s and 1790s from his retirement in the country. Relatively little read today, his long poems describe nature with truth and tenderness, well suited for reading aloud in the evening circle, as the Austens did. Jane Austen was bewitched by them, lines and passages running through her head all her life to emerge both light-heartedly and seriously in her letters and novels. "I could not do without a Syringa, for the sake of Cowper's line," she said when planning a garden.

Though uncontroversial, Cowper's poetry is not bland. Afflicted with deep feelings of unworthiness, his vision of life was coloured by his belief in the doctrine of predestination, and his conviction that he was not one of those chosen by God for salvation. Such a pessimistic outlook – he thought the human condition fundamentally an unhappy one – might seem highly antithetical to Jane Austen's positive and predominantly sunny vision. In fact there was much about him with which she was in complete sympathy. They shared a hatred of affectation and cant and a love of the countryside, which was more than merely a preference for fresh air and pleasant scenery.

Cowper's most famous line is "God made the country, and man made the town". This is reminiscent of a remark made by Mrs Austen in a letter of 1770, after a visit to London: " 'tis a sad place, I would not live in it on any account: one has not time to do one's duty either to God or man". Cowper believed that only in the isolation of the countryside could the individual properly examine his own conscience; that the contemplation of nature could arouse the deepest religious feelings; and that God's design was most apparent in natural phenomena – this last a widespread eighteenth century belief, before the challenge posed by Darwin's theories of evolution.

Whether Jane Austen had already formed these views, perhaps from her parents, and was delighted to find them given such fine expression in Cowper; or whether he first made her think on such subjects, there is no other writer, either of poetry or prose, with whom she is in such complete harmony of belief in the fundamental issues of existence. He must be the most important literary influence upon her. She gives her love of Cowper to two of her heroines, Marianne Dashwood and Fanny Price. Marianne says that his beautiful lines have often driven her wild; the calmer Fanny quotes from him directly twice, and her whole nature seems permeated with his philosophy.

Wordsworth & Romanticism

Jane Austen was born five years after William Wordsworth, three after Samuel Taylor Coleridge. Their joint book, *Lyrical Ballads*, came out in 1798, the very same year that we know the Austens purchased a copy of Cowper's complete works, though they were almost certainly already familiar with his poems. There is no mention of the purchase of *Lyrical Ballads*, which was so popular that further editions came out in 1800 and 1802. Of course, lack of documentary evidence does not mean that the Austens did not possess, or borrow and read, this new poetry. But what is certain is that there is no echo of the work of either poet in Jane Austen's writing. She does mention Wordsworth once by name, in the late fragment *Sanditon*. But as it is the foolish Sir Edward Denham, in raving about poetry, who exclaims "Wordsworth has the true soul of it," that rather indicates distance than endorsement.

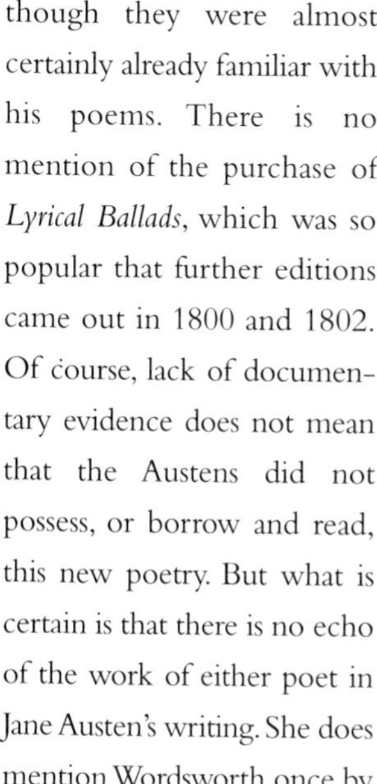

WILLIAM COWPER BY GEORGE ROMNEY, 1792.

In so far as Wordsworth writes out of a great love of nature, and a belief in its regenerative qualities for the spirit of man, she might be expected to admire him. There is much in the Wordsworthian philosophy which is close to that of Cowper. But the fact that *Lyrical Ballads* was thought by the contemporary public to break new ground indicates a fundamental change of emphasis. It treated "humble and rustic life" in simple language and it celebrated mystical and visionary insights which defied rational explanation. The two poets, who had recently planned to set up an idealistic commune in America, held egalitarian political ideas alien to Jane Austen's thinking. It would seem that she was more comfortable with the ideas of her father's contemporary, than with those of her own.

The Novel

"GREAT NOVEL-READERS and not ashamed of being so," Jane Austen once described her family. From her earliest consciousness she was accustomed to hearing novels read aloud, and discussed, in the family circle. Her own first attempts at writing were burlesques and parodies of what she read. The novels available to her fell into two classes. There were the great works of the mid-eighteenth century, all by men. And there were the minor novels in a variety of sub-genres being published throughout her own life by a multitude of authors, predominantly women. Jane Austen read, and relished, all that came her way, sometimes admiring, sometimes ridiculing, but always exercising her fine literary judgement.

HORACE WALPOLE SITTING INSIDE HIS "GOTHICK" MANSION AT STRAWBERRY HILL.

The history of the novel

Poetry and drama had long histories, but the novel, as its name suggested, was relatively new. It had sprung up to answer the need of a class of leisured and literate people who had never before lived in such close social relationship with one another: people who wanted to see their new types of experience reflected and interpreted for them. When Jane Austen's parents were born, in the 1730s, the novel was not yet established on the literary scene; by the time of her own birth, forty years later, its first fine flowering was over. This comprised all the works of the great names of eighteenth-century fiction: Daniel Defoe, Samuel Richardson, Henry Fielding, Lawrence Sterne and Tobias Smollett, the last of whose novels was published in 1771. For the next real fictional masterpiece the public had to wait forty years, for Jane Austen's own first publication in 1811.

So with what did the novel-reading public satisfy its appetite for the new art form between *Humphrey Clinker* and *Sense and Sensibility*? There was no shortage of novels being published, bought, borrowed and read. Novel-reading was now an established habit with a large section of the population, a habit booksellers and circulating libraries were happy to feed. The current practitioners of the craft were either unable to write, or chose not to write, within the realist tradition, producing fiction that aimed to be more exciting than real life. Because of this, and probably too because women had dared to join the ranks of novelists, novels came to be regarded as frivolous, even dangerous to the minds of the young women who were generally supposed to form most of their readership. This was cant, and accounts for Jane Austen's remark about not being ashamed, and for her eloquent defence of the novel in *Northanger Abbey*.

The gothic novel

Horace Walpole, Matthew Lewis, Ann Radcliffe and Regina Roche were the most popular of the novelists working within this genre, which is pilloried heavily in *Northanger Abbey*. Gothic Novels were usually set abroad, in remote and mountainous regions, with ruined castles and abbeys, grisly skeletons, dark mysteries, desperate villains and swooning heroines. They aimed to produce delicious thrills of horror in their readers, as they do in Catherine Morland.

The sentimental novel

The hero or heroine of the sentimental novel feels things more acutely than anybody else. Tears are shed, deaths occur from grief or joy; the Sentimental novel is full of exaggerated emotions, such as Jane

Austen parodied in *Love and Freindship* and, to some extent, in the character of Marianne Dashwood, who aims for the same kind of emotional elitism. Plots are hugely improbable, working on the readers' own emotions with kidnapped babies, tearful partings and reunions, death-bed repentance, wild grief, dead mothers, and any other harrowing circumstance that could be thought up. "A crying volume brings me more money in six months than a heavy merry thing will do in six years," as a bookseller of the time remarked. Titles usually contained either the word Sorrows, Feelings or Heart to indicate the contents.

Fanny Burney

Between Smollett and Jane Austen, the most important novelist was probably Fanny Burney. Her novel *Evelina* was published in 1778, when she was twenty-six, and was an immediate, huge success. The tale of a young lady's entrance into the world, it is still readable today for its high spirits and gallery of fools and rogues. Burney's next two novels, *Cecilia* of 1782 and *Camilla* of 1796, are more laboured, but still the nearest thing to pictures of true life and female tribulations in the real world until Jane Austen herself. Jane Austen certainly read, enjoyed and learnt from Fanny Burney, and quoted from her, or alluded to her characters, more often than she did of any other novelist. *Camilla*, which was expressly written to make enough money to build a house after Fanny Burney had married a penniless French emigré, was published on the subscription system, whereby buyers paid their money before publication, and if there were enough of them to make it viable, had the pleasure of seeing their names printed in the book. "Miss J. Austen of Steventon" was one of the subscribers to *Camilla* – which in using the phrase "pride and prejudice" several times in its closing pages, gave the young subscriber an alternative name for her own "First Impressions".

MADAME D'ARBLAY, FANNY BURNEY.

ILLUSTRATION FROM SIR WALTER SCOTT'S "WAVERLEY", WHICH JANE AUSTEN READ IN 1814.

The Rights of Woman

OPPOSITE: MARY WOLLSTONECRAFT BY JOHN OPIE, 1797.

THE ENLIGHTENED and rational nature of eighteenth-century thought was conducive to the first wave of feminism. For in a society where morals and manners are being debated as important issues, it was natural that certain intellectual women should seek a part in the debate and should question, in particular, why women should not be considered as fully rational beings, with the same moral stature as men.

THE ACTRESS MRS JORDAN, WHO DEFIED THE CONVENTIONS THAT RESTRICTED WOMEN'S PLACE IN SOCIETY.

These early "female philosophers" as they were then called, or feminists as we would term them today, were non-militant and concerned only with rooting out male prejudice by rational argument. They made no demands for legal or constitutional change in the status of women. What blue-stocking authors like Mary Astell, Lady Mary Chudleigh and Catherine Macaulay discussed in their essays and pamphlets were questions of female education, marriage, moral autonomy and authority within the family. These are precisely the issues with which Jane Austen was to concern herself in her novels, which certainly, in their sympathetic portrayals of female lives, and claims for full moral stature in her female characters, bear a feminist reading. Meanwhile a more colourful and controversial figure had burst upon the feminist scene.

Mary Wollstonecraft

A teacher, novelist and outspoken polemical writer, who lived out her life in accordance with her unconventional principles, Mary Wollstonecraft did more for female emancipation in the long run than her more ladylike predecessors. Yet she was also, unwittingly, the cause of a serious setback in the movement, from which it took a very long time to recover.

Her most famous work is *A Vindication of the Rights of Woman*, which was published in 1792, when Jane Austen was at the most impressionable age of sixteen, though we do not know whether a copy ever came her way. It seems unlikely that she could not have read it if she wished to, as she was a member of various book clubs and circulating libraries over the next few years.

A Vindication ... sums up the feminist ideas that had been developing over the century, and places them in the context of post-revolutionary Europe, in itself a dangerous ploy. By acknowledging her radical sympathies, the author risked alienating many, like Jane Austen herself, who would not otherwise fault her reasoning. The book emphasizes that reason and rational principle are the best guides to conduct in all human beings, male or female. It attacks male icons, particularly Milton and Rousseau, for advocating submission and weakness in women as a means of appealing to men. One of her main arguments is that the education girls receive equips them to attract husbands, but not to make good wives and mothers: "The civilized women of the present century, with a few exceptions, are only anxious to inspire love, when they ought to cherish a nobler ambition, and by their abilities and virtues exact respect."

The 1798 controversy

Six years after the publication of *A Vindication* ... , Mary Wollstonecraft died in giving birth to her daughter Mary Godwin, who was to become the wife of the poet Shelley and author of *Frankenstein*.

A few months after her death, Mary Wollstonecraft's husband, the radical writer William Godwin, published a *Memoir* of her. With genuine respect for the truth, but foolish disregard for how the truth would be received, he revealed the so-called "irregularities" in his wife's life story: a love affair that resulted in the birth of an illegitimate child, suicide attempts, and the conception of their own child before marriage.

As a result, Mary Wollstonecraft was branded a whore and an atheist – Godwin had exaggerated her rejection of Christianity to suit his own views – and not only her own arguments discredited, but those of any other woman who dared to write on the subject, for it was argued they all wanted to overthrow the institutions of marriage and religion. It would be half a century before the feminist movement found its voice again.

Meanwhile, to add to their difficulties in trying to gain respect for their work in a male-dominated sphere, women writers of any kind, even those not addressing feminist issues, had to be more careful than ever to stress their respectable private lives, domestic virtues and ladylike credentials.

As part of the angry male response to Godwin's revelations, within the year the Reverend Richard Polwhele had published an anti-feminist satirical poem entitled *The Unsex'd Females*. He put forward the view that it was a sign of the corruption of the age that women's work should be considered on its merits, like men's. He described "the sparkle of confident intelligence" as, in itself, a proof of immodesty in a female author.

1798 was the year that, had the publisher Cadell accepted Mr Austen's offer of his daughter's manuscript the previous November, *First Impressions*, that most "light and bright and sparkling" of all novels, would have first appeared. Was there an element of relief in Jane Austen's natural disappointment? It would be five years before she would even attempt to sell any of her finished manuscripts again.

CHAPTER FOUR

The Visual World

WHATEVER MAY HAVE BEEN the practical and social difficulties of living in Jane Austen's world; whatever may have been the drawbacks to temper the delights in any comparative survey of her age and our own; one thing is certain, visually, her world was beautiful. Nature was tamed but not despoiled. The landscape of England and all that adorned it had never been lovelier. Everything designed by man, from a cup to a carriage, from a gown to a townscape, was fashioned with delicacy, proportion and fitness for purpose. It seemed that nobody, even the humblest village craftsman, could make anything ugly, so well were ideas about visual taste developed and agreed among the whole community. The result was that all the elements that make up a visual environment worked well together; nothing jarred.

It is this world of loveliness that is so bewitching when one of her novels is recreated on film. In this medium, we can forget bad smells, squalor, toothache, and fear of dying in childbirth. We can forget that had we lived then, we probably would not have had the right to vote and we certainly would not have had electricity or modern plumbing.

We can sit back and allow ourselves to be ravished through our eyes. "The England of that time," as A.L. Rowse has said, "makes the heart ache to think of". Of course, stretches of landscape and houses of the period remain, and can be visited and enjoyed. But only on film can this lost and lovely England, peopled in the appropriate costume and carriages, unspoilt by cars and double yellow lines, be effectively recaptured.

A point worth pondering is that it would be unthinkable to set any dramatization of a Jane Austen novel in a period other than the Regency. Shakespeare, for example, works well in many kinds of dress, including modern; but Jane Austen is totally of her time. The appearance of her world and its mores and manners – the stuff of her novels – are closely bound up together.

Again, we find the fascinating changes and developments between the late eighteenth century and the early nineteenth, which we have traced in the society and spirit of the age, reflected also in details of the visual world. In painting as in poetry, the Romantic movement altered the subjects the artist wished to treat, as well as the treatment itself. Even the clothes people wore became more romantic, loose and flowing.

In the applied arts – architecture, landscape gardening, town planning – which affected people's domestic circumstances, show gave way to comfort; public considerations to private ones. The Georgian town house in London, Edinburgh or Bath is separated from the public pavement only by railings and steps; the principal rooms face the street and the facade is indistinguishable from its neighbours, since they wish, collectively, to be taken for one great mansion. The ordinary Regency house, by contrast, is a semi-detached villa with a little garden round three sides; it is made for privacy, cosy domesticity and that happiest of all compromises, *rus in urbe*: one's own bit of country in the town

How interested was Jane Austen herself in the visual environment? She certainly had a deep appreciation of natural scenery, remarking that her idea of heaven was a beautiful landscape. "It was a sweet view," runs the famous line in *Emma*. "sweet to the mind and to the eye. English verdure, English culture, English comfort... ". However, she makes few remarks and virtually no aesthetic judgments about paintings, buildings or furnishings. Two explanations are possible. One is that since everything was so uniformly pleasing, she took good design in man-made objects for granted. The other explanation she offered herself on the occasion of a rare visit to an art gallery in London. "Mary and I," she wrote, "went to the Liverpool Museum & the British Gallery, & I had some amusement at each, tho' my preference for Men & Women, always inclines me to attend more to the company than the sight."

A Very English Art

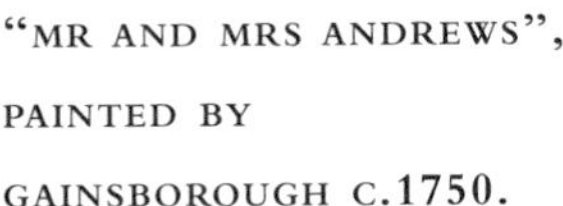

"MR AND MRS ANDREWS", PAINTED BY GAINSBOROUGH C.1750.

JANE AUSTEN'S OPPORTUNITIES for looking at paintings were mainly confined to those hanging on the walls of the many houses she visited. Family portraits predominated. When Elizabeth Bennet is shown round Pemberley by the housekeeper Mrs Reynolds, "In the gallery there were many family portraits, but they could have little to fix the attention of a stranger," and Elizabeth walks on in quest of the only face she can recognize, Mr Darcy's. Similarly, at Sotherton Court, "Of pictures there were abundance, and some few good, but the larger part were family portraits, no longer any thing to any body but Mrs Rushworth, who had been at great pains to learn all that the housekeeper could teach, and was now almost equally well qualified to show the house." These passages suggest that family portraits were the eighteenth century equivalent of today's holiday slides – forced on visitors and often found tiresome.

In *Persuasion*, the parlour of the Great House at Uppercross is adorned with pictures of "gentlemen in brown velvet and ladies in blue satin, who seem to be "staring in astonishment" at the fashionable disorder in the room, introduced by the daughters of the house.

Patronage and pastoral

The vast majority of eighteenth century family portraits were, of course, painted by second- and third-rate provincial portrait painters. Most sitters would have been quite satisfied as long as they could detect a likeness and put on their walls something that confirmed their self-importance.

Those who could appreciate and afford first-rate painters for their portraits commissioned Reynolds, Gainsborough, Romney and, toward the end of the century, Thomas Lawrence. Among Romney's patrons were Thomas and Catherine Knight of Godmersham, the couple who adopted Jane's brother Edward. Because so many people wanted – and could afford – their faces recorded for posterity, portraiture was the most profitable genre in the eighteenth century.

The most expressive portraitists, or those who wanted to paint more than just faces, placed their sitters among their possessions, either in or out of doors. Perhaps the most famous of such pictures is Thomas Gainsborough's *Mr and Mrs Andrews*, in which the couple occupy only the left hand side of the picture, while the remainder is given over to their country estate, with fields of ripening corn and flocks of sheep. It is a blissful pastoral vision, and though it comes half a century before, it anticipates Emma's complacent view of Abbey Mill Farm, in "all its appendages of prosperity and beauty, its rich pastures, spreading flocks, orchard in blossom and light column of smoke ascending ...".

Sir Joshua Reynolds, who founded the Royal Academy in 1768, sometimes clothed his sitters in drapes and posed them as figures from classical mythology, though the misty landscape that they inhabit remains detectably English. Both he and Gainsborough, by developing their personal visions of the pastoral, attempted to raise portraiture to the level of the highest art, while working within the confines of patronage. That these artists were so successful in worldly terms is because they caught the mood of their times in their depiction of a cultivated upper class inhabiting a cultivated land.

A different landscape

Joseph Mallord William Turner, born 1775, and John Constable, born 1776, were exact contemporaries of Jane Austen, as well as of the Romantic poets. Theirs was a new vision of England, shaped by a post-revolutionary ideology. Both in subject matter and technique, they were innovators.

Not least of the changes between them and their predecessors was that they painted for themselves, not for the market. For centuries art had been made for patrons, whether the church, the crown or the wealthy individual. The idea of the artist starving in his garret for the sake of the integrity of his art was one of the inventions of the Romantic movement. "Dear John," as Mrs Constable wrote to him in 1809, "how much I do wish your profession prove more lucrative. When will the time come that you realize!!!"

Constable was like Wordsworth in choosing humble country people and occupations as the subjects of his art. The public were scandalized that he should dare to paint large canvases on these themes. Constable was like Wordsworth too in seeking to discover himself and his origins in all his work.

His roughness of technique with its dancing dots and flecks of light, and Turner's vaporous atmospheric washes, were equally suspect to those who expected high finish in high art. This experimentation began in the decade which saw Jane Austen at the height of her creative powers; in a curious parallel, her last work, *Sanditon*, replicates these impressionistic techniques in words, a new departure for her. The bulk of Constable's and Turner's work was to come after Jane Austen's death, for though born within a year of her they both long outlived her. Between them, Constable and Turner reinvented and democratized English art.

"WEYMOUTH BAY" BY CONSTABLE, C.1816.

The Picturesque

IN HIS BRIEF Biographical Notice of his sister, Henry Austen tells us that she was "early enamoured of Gilpin on the Picturesque". What does this mean?

Gilpin

"LANDSCAPE WITH A RUINED CASTLE", BY GILPIN.

William Gilpin was a clergyman, schoolmaster and amateur artist of north country origins who lived in the New Forest area of Hampshire. He invented the term "picturesque" in relation to natural scenery, saying "We precisely mean by it, that kind of beauty that would look good in a picture". From the 1770s he made a series of tours in the remoter parts of the British Isles, describing, drawing and assessing the scenery according to his notions of the Picturesque. His books, in order of publication, were:

The Wye and South Wales, 1782
The Lakes, 1789
Forest Scenery, 1791
The West of England and the Isle of Wight, 1798
The Highlands, 1800

They therefore exactly span the period of Jane Austen's youthful reading, from about the age of seven to twenty-five. They were very influential in giving her an idea of the different regions of her own country and the variety of scenery to be found there. And not only Jane Austen. Gilpin opened the eyes of the British people generally to the beauties of their own land. Areas furthest from the centres of civilization, that had seemed featureless, hostile and fit only for a few miserable peasants to eke a poor living, now began to be celebrated for their wildness and grandeur. Almost single-handedly Gilpin created a craze for travel in the British educated classes.

Before Gilpin, nobody had valued unproductive nature for its purely aesthetic qualities. For centuries man had been battling to wrest the means of subsistence from nature, but it was only when the ingenuity and agricultural advances of the Georgians had given them a measure of control over her caprices and secured them a comfortable lifestyle that they could allow themselves the thrill of relishing her power and splendour. In other words, bodily needs having been satisfied, they now looked to nature to nourish their souls as well.

The jargon of the Picturesque

In forming his pictures, Gilpin looked for intricate foregrounds, with rocks, moss, brushwood and tree stumps, nettles and thistles. Trees were useful as sidescreens to the picture, middle distances ought to be irregular and rugged, and far distances are best when softened by a hazy atmosphere. Cattle, when they appear, should be in groups of three or five, never four. Ploughed fields were against the spirit of the picturesque, and hovels and ruins were preferable to tidy farmhouses. So well had all these strictures entered the consciousness of the nation by the 1790s, that they were become, according to Marianne Dashwood, who is an ardent disciple of Gilpin, "a mere jargon".

Greatly though she enjoyed Gilpin's writing, Jane Austen, being never slow to spot an absurdity, could not take him entirely seriously. She knew that Britain's agricultural prosperity was among the country's greatest assets, especially at time of war. In any case, she found the farmed landscape very beautiful. So when Gilpin writes off the whole of the interior of Devon as "an uninteresting scene" and claims that the Isle of Wight is "disfigured by the spade, the coulter and the harrow"; and when he goes on to say, without regard for the fact that people must have bread to eat, that "the regularity of cornfields disgusts, and the colour of corn, especially near harvest, is out of tune with everything else," she sends the Dashwood family to live in the interior of Devon and has Edward Ferrars tease Marianne about both the jargon and the ideas:

> *Remember I have no knowledge of the picturesque, and I shall offend you if we come to particulars. I shall call hills steep, which ought to be bold; surfaces strange and uncouth, which ought to be irregular and rugged; and distant objects out of sight, which ought only to be indistinct through the soft medium of a hazy atmosphere. I call it a very fine country – the hills are steep, the woods seem full of fine timber, and the valley looks comfortable and snug – with rich meadows and several neat farm houses scattered here and there. It exactly answers my idea of a fine country, because it unites beauty with utility – and I dare say it is a picturesque one too...*

So much was Gilpin part of Jane Austen's mental furniture, that all three of the Steventon novels contain some response to him. In *Pride and Prejudice* Elizabeth Bennet, declining an invitation to join the Bingley sisters and Mr Darcy in a walk, jokes, "You are charmingly group'd, and appear to uncommon advantage. The picturesque would be spoilt by admitting a fourth." Later she enthuses about the projected tour to the Lakes in Gilpinesque terms.

In *Northanger Abbey* the Tilneys and Catherine Morland take a walk to Beechen Cliff, from where they can see the city spread beneath them. The Tilneys are used to looking at scenery with an eye to drawing, and talk in phrases that mean nothing to her.

When she confesses her ignorance, Henry gives Catherine her first lesson in picturesque principles:

> *He talked of foregrounds, distances, and second distances – sidescreens and perspectives – light and shades; – and Catherine was so hopeful a scholar, that when they gained the top of Beechen Cliff, she voluntarily rejected the whole city of Bath, as unworthy to make part of a landscape.*

A PICTURESQUE SCENE AT STONELEIGH PARK. VISITED BY JANE AUSTEN IN 1806.

Landscape Gardening

An especially English contribution to European culture, landscape gardening was one of the arts in which Jane Austen was most keenly interested. By the time she was growing up at Steventon the rage for "improvements", as they were often known, had percolated down to people with quite modest gardens, such as her own parents, and the literature of garden theory had become part of every educated person's mental equipment.

THE TEMPLE OF APOLLO AT STOURHEAD, WILTSHIRE.

The earliest improvers were the aristocrats, great landowners, poets and essayists who remodelled their grounds after returning from the Grand Tour of the Continent where they had been inspired by the landscape paintings of Poussin and Claude. Previously, the greatest gardens of the land had been composed of straight lines, symmetrical parterres, canals and avenues, all highly artificial and designed to show man's mastery over nature. In estate after estate, these were all swept away, and the garden made to look like part of the natural landscape. This was made possible by the invention of the ha-ha, or sunken ditch, which kept deer or cattle out of the garden but made no interruption in the view. Horace Walpole, one of the eighteenth century's most prolific writers on gardening, called the invention of the ha-ha "this simple enchantment". To demonstrate their erudition, the early improvers often adorned their grounds with classical buildings and statuary, as can be seen at Stourhead and Stowe.

Capability Brown

The first great professional of landscape gardening was Lancelot Brown, who gained his famous nickname by seeing the "capabilities" for improvement in the parks he was called on to refashion. Brown composed his gardens out of the simplest components: flowing lawns, clumps of trees and expanses of shining water. To achieve the right effects on the grand scale in which he worked, huge amounts of earth would have to be moved, creating informal contours and persuading small streams to turn into lakes.

Brown was active from about 1740 to his death in 1783. "I have not yet finished England," he is reported to have said when offered £1,000 to look

"THE SUPERB LILY" BY ROBERT JOHN THORNTON, 1799.

at the "capabilities" of Ireland. A representative Brown creation was the park at Chatsworth, home of the Duke of Devonshire, in Derbyshire, which is visited by Elizabeth Bennet and the Gardiners on their northern tour. Pemberley itself, Mr Darcy's estate in the same county, sounds very Brownian in its design: "It was a large, handsome, stone building, standing well on rising ground, and backed by a ridge of high, woody hills; and in front, a stream of some natural importance was swelled into greater, but without any artificial appearance. Its banks were neither formal, nor falsely adorned." However, Brown had his critics:

Oft when I've seen some lonely mansion stand,
Fresh from th'improver's desolating hand,
'Midst shaven lawns, that far around it creep
In one eternal undulating sweep . . .

wrote Richard Payne Knight in *The Landscape of 1794*, going on to call for a return of "some features ... to break this uniform, eternal green". The next fashion in landscape gardening would do just that.

Humphry Repton

Mentioned by Jane Austen in *Mansfield Park*, a novel that includes much discussion of improvements, Humphry Repton developed Brown's ideas to suit the rather different requirements of the next generation. While remaining fluid and natural, Repton's parks and gardens introduced more variety into the scene, both as a response to the picturesque movement, and because his clients demanded greater convenience and comfort from their grounds. Instead of immediately stepping out onto lawn, they now wanted a gentler and more practical transition between house and garden. So Repton introduced the ballustraded terrace, the conservatory and the trellis-covered walk.

Mrs Austen's rich relations called in Repton to remodel the garden at Adlestrop in Gloucestershire. In the same county, Repton also worked on the Blaise Castle estate, giving it a winding carriage drive and a picturesque rustic building in the form of a woodman's cottage, to be glimpsed in the distance with its plume of smoke. Colour had been banished from the great parks by Brown, but toward the turn of the century interest in flowers revived, stimulated by exotic new varieties being brought back from all parts of the globe. The flower garden newly created for Fanny Dashwood when she becomes mistress of Norland, Lady Bertram's flower garden at Mansfield and Elizabeth Elliot's "own sweet flower garden" at Kellynch are three examples in the novels of this new source of genteel female pleasure. Of course, cottagers and the minor gentry, like the Austens themselves, had gone on cultivating flowers amidst their vegetables and herbs all through the century, not being quite such slaves to fashion as the owners of the great country estates.

While Jane Austen was in sympathy with many of Repton's ideas, and also admired the Brownian landscape when the size of the place warranted a grand treatment, she retained a sneaking affection for gardens that had escaped the changes of fashion.

HUMPHRY REPTON AT WORK.

The Country House

OF ALL LOVELY THINGS created in the Georgian era, the country house was undoubtedly the loveliest. The Georgians had a genius for building. Money and taste were both in good supply. As a consequence their legacy to us includes countless number of Palladian houses, great and small, made of stone or brick, distinguished by their exquisite symmetry and proportion. It was a style equally well suited to the imposing mansion of a great landowner, set in its rolling parkland, as to a more modest dwelling like a country rectory. Such a building might be only five windows wide above, with a central front door and two windows on the ground floor either side, but on that scale it would possess all the charm of a doll's house.

Jane Austen's intimacy with such houses, of all sizes, was extensive, from Godmersham Park, the splendid 1730s-built home of her brother Edward, to Ibthorpe House in Hampshire, rented for a while by her friends the Lloyds, a delightful brick-built specimen of the medium-sized Georgian house.

GODMERSHAM PARK HOME OF JANE AUSTEN'S BROTHER EDWARD AND OFTEN VISITED BY HER.

Calm and authoritative, the Palladian style perfectly expressed the spirit of a self-confident and ordered age. Almost all the houses in which Jane Austen places her characters would have been in this style. The only exceptions are when she tells us specifically that a house is older – Sotherton Court, for example, is Elizabethan – or exceptionally new, like Trafalgar House in *Sanditon*. Her fictional houses have no direct counterparts in real life. Rather they were products of her imagination, taking this and that feature from from the wealth of those known to her.

Regency Styles

When the restrained perfection of the classical style eventually began to seem exhausted, or insipid, later generations of Georgian and Regency builders sought variety by adding frolics and flourishes inspired by the Oriental, Greek Revival or Gothic influence. Where once there had been only one acceptable architecture, now there was a confusion of styles to choose from. The Royal Pavilion at Brighton, built as a classical villa 1780, was given its fantastic onion-domed dress by John Nash in 1815, and was only the most flamboyant of several early eighteenth century buildings in this style. The characteristic of the Greek Revival house was the Doric portico, but it was a rather grave style more often applied to public buildings than houses.

High Gothic was eventually to monopolize architecture whether for public, domestic or ecclesiastical buildings, but this was later in the nineteenth century. Regency Gothic was more playful and more superficial. Its pointed windows were applied to houses of otherwise classical symmetry. Even the

KEDLESTON HALL IN DERBYSHIRE AN ELEGANT EXAMPLE OF A NEO-CLASSICAL COUNTRY HOUSE, DESIGNED BY ROBERT ADAM.

window that was added to Chawton Cottage in 1809 was given Gothic glazing bars, though the house had been built a century before. Regency Gothic, which might also feature toy turrets and battlements, was especially favoured for houses by the sea.

Two favourite decorative building materials of the Regency period were stucco and wrought iron, both of which gave a light and cheerful look to the houses they adorned. Wrotham Rectory in Kent, where Jane Austen spent two nights in 1813 as the guest of some relations of her brother Edward, makes generous use of both. This charming small house might have been the model for Uppercross Cottage in *Persuasion*, with its iron "veranda and other prettinesses".

Abbeys, castles and follies

One kind of country house was quite different from any of these. There was a taste for antiquity throughout the period which made owners of genuine old abbeys and castles particularly envied. Many abbeys had survived the Reformation to be converted into homes for the aristocracy or gentry. Examples in the novels include Donwell Abbey and Northanger Abbey, both in their different ways made into comfortable homes. Catherine Morland, with her "passion for ancient edifices" caught from reading gothic novels, thrills at the idea of staying in a real abbey, only to find to her very great disappointment that it has been thoroughly modernized and extended with classical wings. Stoneleigh Abbey in Warwickshire, seat of Mrs Austen's family the Leighs, had undergone a similar treatment, a massive Baroque block having been added to the original medieval structure, with no attention paid to consistency of style. Donwell Abbey has been more sympathetically handled. Its rooms are "rambling and irregular" suggesting no modern additions.

When Georgian landowners longed for some relic of antiquity to call their own, they often set about building one themselves to add interest to their grounds. Thus Blaise Castle, which John Thorpe tells Catherine Morland is the oldest castle in the land, was actually built in 1766. Jane Austen would have expected her readers to know that it was merely a garden folly, designed to look good from the windows of Blaise Castle House, itself a very restrained Palladian mansion. Blaise is a fully finished but miniature castle; other follies were actually built as ruins.

About the building of ruins, William Gilpin wrote, "To give the stone its mouldering appearance ... to show how correspondent parts have once united, though now the chasm runs wide between them, and to scatter heaps of ruin around with negligence and ease, are great efforts of art." And then, he added, if weather and nature do not play their part, "Your ruin will be still incomplete - you may as well write over the gate, 'Built in the year 1772' ". His advice that a man should not attempt to build a ruin unless he had £30,000 to spend is an exaggeration. But the nation that could afford the money and ingenuity to build ruins, certainly must have enjoyed a superfluity of both.

Interiors

THE INTERIOR OF KENWOOD HOUSE, HAMPSTEAD, NORTH LONDON.

FROM ABOUT THE 1770S came a change in the interior layout of the large country house. Early eighteenth century mansions had been designed to impress visitors with a series of state rooms opening out of one another, forming, when all the intervening doors were open, a long vista. But increasingly the comfort, enjoyment and privacy of the family became paramount, and in modern houses rooms each with their separate purpose opened off a central hall – drawing room, dining room, library, billiard room and so forth.

Whereas once the principal rooms had occupied the *piano nobile* – a raised storey above the semi-basement kitchen and offices – in the more modern houses they were sited on the ground floor, so that family and guests could step easily into the garden. At about the turn of the century, French windows became popular, and conservatories and verandahs were later introduced to make the transition from house to garden even more tempting.

The spirit of the home

Within the rooms, the arrangement of the furniture was also changing. It was now scattered informally in pleasant groupings, instead of being ranged against the walls and brought forward by servants when required. This is what is happening to the old-fashioned square parlour at Uppercross, "to which the present daughters of the house were gradually giving the proper air of confusion by a grand piano forte and a harp, flower-stands and little tables placed in every direction". The lived-in look was fashionable. Needlework, books and letters could be left scattered about; without such evidence of feminine occupation, as the novelist Fanny Burney remarked in 1801, "a room always looks forlorn".

Indeed, Jane Austen's lifetime witnessed a feminization of the home in spirit as well as visual detail. From being a rather masculine area of pomp and display, in which women's concerns had little place, it became the setting for cosy domesticity where men might look to women for their soothing and civilising influence. Home became the woman's acknowledged domain. It took the Victorians to invent the concept of the "Angel of the House" – the guardian of unsullied morality within the sacred home. But Regency families were certainly taking the first steps in that direction. Sir Thomas Bertram, in wishing to "shut out noisy pleasures" and spend every evening seated round the hearth with his womenfolk, is a straw in the wind.

Furnishing Styles

Lightness, elegance and a diversity of influences characterized Regency interiors as well as exteriors. Gothic, Greek and Oriental details might be applied to furniture as much as to architecture, though not necessarily in the same house. There was a fourth very fashionable style, the Egyptian, which was inspired by Nelson's defeat of Napoleon at the Battle of the Nile in 1798.

A Regency room would contain more pieces of furniture, and objects generally, than a mid-Georgian one, but each piece would be more delicate, even spindly. Sheraton was the most famous cabinet-maker of the 1790s and early 1800s; he died in 1806. The six-legged sideboard (four in the front and two at the back) was his invention. Ovals, a favourite Sheraton motif, were much used in inlay. Characteristic designs of the period included the X-framed stool and the Grecian sofa, designed to be seen from the back as well as the front, since it might be placed in the middle of the room. Reclining on a sofa was itself a Regency idea, shocking to the older generation who had been trained to sit bolt upright on settees and chairs.

Fireplaces gave scope for elegant design. On the mantelpiece might be ornaments of "the prettiest English china" as there are at Northanger Abbey. A large mirror over the fireplace reflected the light from an increasing number of candelabra back into the room. Dark wooden floors were now more likely to be covered either in carpet, or the newly invented oilcloth, forerunner of linoleum. Wallpaper became cheaper towards the end of the eighteenth century, and the striped and floral designs in pastel colours also added to the impression of lightness in rooms. Windows were larger, glazing bars thinner, and drapes made of lightweight fabrics.

AN ORMOLU-MOUNTED MAHOGANY WINDOW SEAT FROM THE REIGN OF GEORGE IV.

An acquisitive society

In any description of the trends of Regency furnishing, however, it must not be forgotten that many, if not most, of the houses Jane Austen visited and wrote about contained furniture from an earlier age, or a mixture of periods. We must not imagine all her interiors being pure Regency, a mistake modern film-makers do not always avoid. But it is true that the diffusion of prosperity, and awareness of fashion, certainly encouraged the replacement and renewal of furniture, furnishings and other objects for the home. Mary Crawford, when she is thinking of marrying Tom Bertram before Edmund takes his place in her affections, considers Mansfield Park "might do" if it were "completely new furnished". Yet Mansfield Park seems modern compared with Sotherton Court, so out of date as to warrant one of Jane Austen's rare descriptions of an interior: "amply furnished in the taste of fifty years back, with shining floors, solid mahogany, rich damask, marble, gilding and carving".

At the time of Elizabeth Bennet's visit to Pemberley, Mr Darcy has newly furnished a pretty sitting room for his sister "with greater elegance and lightness" than the remainder of the house. Willoughby hints at buying "modern furniture" for Allenham, when it becomes his own, at a cost of about £200 per room. Old furniture was not valued, even sentimentalists like Marianne Dashwood desired to possess the latest styles.

WALLPAPER OF THE ERA.

The Fashionable Spa

THE FASHION FOR TAKING the waters and enjoying all the social amenities that a spa town could offer was established well before Jane Austen's birth, but was still very much part of her world. Bath, of course, was the original spa resort. For many decades in the middle of the century it was the only fashionable place to go for people who could afford a little variety from home. Royalty, aristocracy, politicians, poets and artists all flocked to Bath, for health and pleasure. Its astonishing growth soon drew rivals who hoped to emulate its prosperity. The north of England developed its own spas, notably Buxton and Harrogate, and in the south-east there was Tunbridge Wells. Cheltenham was a late arrival on the scene, and was visited by Jane Austen toward the end of her life; but it was Bath she knew intimately, both as a place and as a social phenomenon.

HUMPHRY REPTON, "THE PUMP ROOM, BATH"

The building of Bath

It is a curious coincidence that one of Jane Austen's forbears on her mother's side – James Brydges, first Duke of Chandos – should have played a crucial role in developing the city which, nearly a hundred years later, she was to immortalize in her novels. He and his second wife, Cassandra Willoughby, were among the early aristocratic visitors to try the thermal waters. They came to Bath in 1727 in quest of relief from his "twitching nerves" and her "hysterical fits". What they found was a city little changed from medieval times, with ramshackle buildings, cramped alleyways and no decent accommodation for visitors of quality.

The Duke was quick to spot an investment opportunity. He was responsible for the first speculative row of terrace houses in Bath. The architect and builder he chose was the then unknown John Wood, who having established his credit-worthiness went on to build on his own account.

Wood conceived grand schemes for turning Bath into a new Roman city, and though not all his schemes came to pass, he laid out North and South Parade with substantial houses and broad pavements, and he built Queen Square, outside the city walls, the grandest piece of town planning of its day (1732). Each side of the Square was designed to look like one imposing mansion. Wood continued building houses up the hilly Gay Street, which opened out into his next set piece, the Circus. Like a Roman amphitheatre turned inside out, the Circus is distinguished by the use of all three classical orders of architecture. Wood's son, John Wood the younger, continued his father's development with Brock Street and the semi-elliptical south-facing Royal Crescent, perhaps the loveliest townscape in all England. It was completed in the year of Jane Austen's birth, and her uncle Edward Cooper took a house there.

If the physical beauty of Bath was due largely to the vision of John Wood, its social character was determined by Richard "Beau" Nash. The wealthy people who came to Bath for six or eight weeks in the season were not just in quest of health from drinking or immersing in the waters. They also wanted to mix socially with people of similar rank, to see and be seen, to promenade by day and dance by night. As the Master of Ceremonies at the Assembly Rooms, Nash formulated and upheld codes of behaviour. His authoritarian rule civilised the coarseness of the aristocracy – he was even known to reprimand the formidable Sarah, Duchess of Marlborough – and formed the manners of the new rich. From Bath these standards were taken back to all corners of the country, creating the homogeneous polite society that existed everywhere by the time Jane Austen was born.

Bath in Jane Austen's day

When Jane Austen paid her first visits in the 1790s, Bath was more popular with more people than ever, but precisely for this reason it had lost its edge of fashion. The upper echelons of society no longer patronized Bath, which was filled with the gentry and middle classes. Physically too the city was still expanding. The built environment of Bath had spread way above the Royal Crescent to the heights of the northern hills – wave upon wave of golden stone terraces, crescents and squares. Pulteney Bridge, by Robert Adam, the only bridge in England to be lined with shops, had carried the development across the river Avon to the Bathwick meadows, opening up a whole new area for building with a level approach to the city. This was where the Austens themselves took a house when Mr Austen retired in 1801. By this date the amenities of Bath – shops, theatres, assembly rooms, libraries and so forth – were making it an attractive place for retirement, and the whole character of the place was becoming more sedate.

Jane Austen gives us two portraits of Bath, separated by about twenty years. *Northanger Abbey* shows us Bath through the eyes of a young woman for whom every sight and every new experience is a fresh matter of wonder. The rituals of the city are still as Beau Nash had decreed; life is lived communally. By the time *Persuasion* was written, that was beginning to change. The house which Sir Walter Elliot takes, in the "lofty and dignified" Camden Place, is very high above the city, indicative of his supercilious attitude toward most of its inhabitants.

Cheltenham

This was the other spa known to Jane Austen. She visited in 1816, when her health was failing, to drink from its cold springs. At this time the city stood poised at the beginning of its boom. A creation of the Regency, Cheltenham had a very different character from Bath, not only architecturally but socially. Unlike the older spa, with its winter season of indoor pleasures, Cheltenham was a summer resort, designed to be enjoyed out of doors. Built in a level location, its streets were more spacious and airy than those of Bath. It had its share of grand terraces, but its detached and semi-detached villas in their individual gardens gave the town much of its semi-rural charm.

THE LEAFY STREETS OF CHELTENHAM, A REGENCY RESORT.

Seaside Resorts

SEA-BATHING WAS FOR the Georgians an extension of spa-bathing. It was popularized in the 1750s by Dr Russell of Brighton, which was then an obscure fishing village called Brighthelmstone. The patronage of the Prince of Wales from the 1780s ensured Brighton's pre-eminence among seaside resorts, especially with the more raffish elements of upper-class society. But just as the Prince and his father the King each favoured a different political party, so each had his favourite seaside resort. The King's was Weymouth. He went there in 1789 to recuperate his health after his dreadful illness of the previous year, and professed himself highly delighted with his treatment. This set the royal stamp of approval on sea-bathing for those who had been doubtful before. It also established Weymouth as a rival resort.

SEA BATHING BECAME FASHIONABLE IN THE LATE EIGHTEENTH CENTURY.

From the 1780s both places began to draw off the most fashionable visitors from Bath. But Brighton and Weymouth had no monopoly on the sea or the shore. Other little villages all along the south coast from Teignmouth in Devon to Margate in Kent thought they were just as good and set about developing themselves to attract the wealthy. Jane Austen visited many of these places, and invented one of her own, Sanditon, in the last piece of fiction she wrote before she died.

Sea-bathing

And all, impatient of dry land, agree
With one consent to rush into the sea.

So wrote Jane Austen's favourite poet, Cowper, of this new craze. Sea-bathing was considered to be safest in the winter, or if that was not possible in the cold of an early morning, when the pores were closed. "We rose at six o'clock in the morn and by the pale blink o' the moon went to the seaside where we had bespoken the bathing-woman to be ready for us, and into the ocean we plunged," wrote the novelist and diarist Fanny Burney from Brighton in November 1782. "It was cold but pleasant. I have bathed so often as to lose my dread of the operation."

Jane's cousin Eliza spent January and February 1791 at Margate for the sake of her sickly little son. A doctor had assured her that "one month's bathing at this time of year was more efficacious than six at any other." Eliza wrote, "The sea has strengthened him wonderfully, and I think has likewise been of great service to myself. I still continue bathing notwithstanding the severity of the weather and frost and snow, which is I think somewhat courageous."

THE ROYAL PAVILION AT BRIGHTON.

Jane Austen herself enjoyed sea-bathing, though in warmer weather. She wrote from Lyme on 14 September 1804, "The bathing was so delightful this morning and Molly so pressing with me to enjoy myself that I believe I stayed in rather too long, as since the middle of the day I have felt unreasonably tired. I shall be more careful another time." There were bathing-machines on the beach at Lyme for use by ladies. The bather would enter one of these machines and be dragged by the bathing-woman – who had, perforce, to be burly – into the sea to about shoulder depth. The bather would descend the steps into the sea, and perhaps be pushed under if she were hesitant. This system preserved the modestly of ladies, who bathed in their clinging muslin shifts for want of any alternative.

In *Persuasion* Mary Musgrove, who is certainly no stoic, enjoys bathing in the latter half of November. But the resort of Lyme is portrayed as "deserted and melancholy" then, the assembly rooms shut up, "the lodgers almost all gone". In season, Jane Austen tells us, the shore is "animated with company." Evidently by 1814, when that novel is set, the season had shifted. People were now visiting the sea not just for the bathing, but for open-air pleasures better enjoyed in smiling weather. September and October were the Austens' own favourite holiday months, though one year at least they were still at the coast as late as the first week in November.

The growth of resorts

All the resorts which vied with one another for visitors had to provide a range of amenities: assembly rooms, shops, a library, medical attendants, a promenade or pleasant walks and, above all, decent accommodation. Brighton and Weymouth had their crescents, squares and terraces like Bath, while pretty little Regency houses, with bow or Gothic windows, and perhaps a balcony or a verandah, were built in the quieter resorts like Dawlish and Sidmouth. The latter place has a particularly fine crop of cottages *ornées*, thatched cottages with decorative detail built not for cottagers but visiting gentry.

In the unfinished *Sanditon* Jane Austen takes a new seaside resort not only as her setting but her subject. The fragment sparkles with the sunshine and sea breezes of which she writes, while tackling a serious concern about the development of the English countryside. Jane Austen shows us the speculators at work, puffing their own resort at the expense of its neighbours, covering the land with new building, opening shops and making every effort to attract just the right number of visitors to make the resort appealing. As a lover of the seaside, she can certainly see its charms. But she could also see that greed and restlessness, if not controlled, might destroy beauty of the England she had been privileged to inhabit.

Transport

HAD SHE EQUALLED her sister and brothers in longevity, Jane Austen would have lived into the age of steam. As it was, it would be nearly thirty years after her death before railways began to have an impact on the English countryside and revolutionize travel for the masses. Her lifespan encompassed the golden age of the horse-drawn carriage and the canal.

"TWO YOUNG LADIES IN CALICO TAKING AN AIRING IN A PHAETON." BY HUMPHRY REPTON.

Carriages

The design and manufacture of carriages reached its apogee in the years of which Jane Austen writes. Vehicles had never been so well-sprung, highly-insulated or streamlined.

The number and stylishness of vehicles owned by a family was as much a matter for self-congratulation or envy as cars are today, especially among the male half of the population. John Thorpe is the notable bore on the subject. He, and almost all the single young men of the novels, drive either a gig or a curricle. Both were lightweight and therefore speedy vehicles, the equivalent of today's sports car, with just two wheels, an open top, and a seat for the owner-driver and one passenger side by side. Thorpe's model is a gig, but is what he calls "curricle-hung", with "seat, trunk, sword-case, splashing-board, lamps and silver moulding," and it cost him fifty guineas (£52.50p).

The coach, the chaise and the chariot were all closed four-wheel vehicles driven by a servant coachman. The coach was the largest vehicle, with two seats facing one another, holding a maximum of six. The chaise and the chariot seated two passengers facing the horses, with an occasional let-down seat for a third, but whereas the driver of the chaise was mounted on one of the horses, the chariot had the addition of a coach-box for his use. Chariots had an especially staid image, associated with elderly ladies.

In the Regency a new class of vehicles was designed to combine the advantages of both open and closed carriages. Choice of such a vehicle is a mark of modernity in the three later novels of Jane Austen, where they are identified with the younger generation like Henry Crawford and Captain Wentworth. The landau is like a coach in its seating arrangements, with the additonal refinement that the roof opened from the middle for use in fine weather. The landaulet resembled the chaise with a one-piece hood that opened from the front and was folded down to the back. The barouche-landau, like the chariot, had a box in front, which could hold the driver and one other.

All these opening vehicles were coveted for summer travelling and "exploring", like that indulged in by the Sucklings in *Emma*, or the party from Mansfield to Sotherton. "What!" as Julia Bertram cries, "go box'd up three in a post-chaise in this weather, when we may have seats in a barouche!"

Canals

The age of inland waterways was inaugurated in 1761 by the opening of the Duke of Bridgwater's canal from his coalfields to Manchester, a distance of seven miles. But it was the years 1790 to 1794 that witnessed canal mania, when Parliament authorized the construction of 81 canals.

Eventually there were to be four thousand miles of canals, linking all the new industrial areas of the Midlands and the North with the four great ports of London, Bristol, Liverpool and Hull. One horse on a canal towpath could draw as much as thirty horses on a road, and one barge could carry up to thirty tons, making it an economic and convenient means of transport for bulky goods like coal, grain, raw materials for industry and manufactured goods. Without the canal system the industrial revolution could hardly have got going, yet the canals were to be made redundant within two generations by the invention of the railways.

Jane Austen, of course, lived far from the industrial heart of Britain, but she was familiar with the country's southernmost canal, the Kennet and Avon, which links the navigable river system from London to Bristol. The Kennet and Avon canal runs from Berkshire to Bath, and Jane witnessed or heard of the construction of both ends of it. At the Berkshire end, it passes through the village of Kintbury, near Newbury, the home of the Austens' friends the Fowles. Construction of the canal began in 1796 and reached Kintbury in 1797, the very year that Cassandra Austen's fiancé Tom Fowle died abroad. The earliest known letter of Jane Austen was written to Cassandra when she was staying at Kintbury Rectory in January 1796, and both sisters were periodic visitors to this lovely, tranquil village over the years.

In Bath the canal was cut through Sydney Gardens, the public pleasure grounds immediately opposite the house in Sydney Place that the Austens occupied from 1801 to 1804. Maps of Bath show that the canal had not reached Sydney Gardens in 1800, but was in place by 1804. The Austens therefore had the opportunity to observe every stage of its construction, and of the beautiful ironwork bridge put in place to reunite the two parts of the divided gardens. In fact the canal enhanced, rather than detracted from, the romantic beauty of the environment, as did almost every artefact the Regency produced.

AQUEDUCT OVER ONE OF THE NEW CANALS OF THE 1790S.

Fashion

LONDON FASHIONS OF 1814.

IT IS NOT TOO GRANDIOSE to claim that fashion in clothes, which might seem such a trivial aspect of life, is closely related to the philosophical and political thinking of an era. Certainly this was true during the lifespan of Jane Austen. Over this period of some forty years, fashion for both men and women was constantly evolving, reflecting the general changes in society. The trend was away from heavy elaborate clothes that testified to the wearer's social standing at the expense of comfort and mobility, to clothes that were lighter, easier to wear, more suitable for informal, English country life. Clothes were still a status symbol – when have they not been – but to be dressed in the height of fashion no longer meant being overburdened with clothes just to demonstrate membership of the leisured classes.

By the first two decades of the nineteenth century, to be fashionable meant to be receptive to new, Romantic ideas about the central importance of the individual. It was not, of course, that most people were making a deliberate statement; but fashion has a mysterious way of evolving in tune with the collective consciousness of the times.

Female dress

The shape of female costume in the 1780s and 1790s, when Jane Austen was growing up and writing the first versions of her novels, was in a state of transition. The waist was rising from its natural place but had not yet reached the point immediately under the bosom from which it could go no higher. A wide sash tied in a bow at the back defined this waistline, above which a crossover style of bodice or ruched muslin neckerchief gave the characteristic pouter pigeon look. Lightweight fabrics in plain subdued colours were favoured in place of the stiff brocades and embroidered silks that had previously been popular. Sashes were often blue, the gown itself peach, coffee or cream-coloured. Hair which had formerly been powdered and piled up to quite fantastic heights (a gift to the caricaturists of the mid-century) was now left *au naturel* and allowed to tumble on to the shoulders in curls.

Out of doors, the new outline was completed by a broad-brimmed hat tied under the chin with a fluttery ribbon. This is the look to which Jane Austen would have aspired as a fashion-conscious young lady making her entrance into local society; and the look which she must have had in mind for her young women as she composed the early versions of *Pride and Prejudice* and *Sense and Sensibility*. No description of what the heroines are wearing is given in either novel, except for the muff carried by Marianne, but it will be remembered that Marianne's hair was "tumbled down her back" when Willoughby cut off a lock.

At about the turn of the century, when Jane

"LES INVISIBLES". SATIRICAL CARTOON BY GILLRAY.

Austen was most exposed to the latest fashions through her residence in Bath, female dress reached one of its periodic extremes. The waist was now very high, the bodice small and plain, skirt straight and often trailing on the floor. Filmy, clinging fabrics such as gauze and muslin revealed the shape of the figure; minimal underclothing was worn to avoid spoiling the line. The look was based on the drapery of Grecian statues, white being the most favoured colour. The Classical Greek influence extended to the hair, which was worn either short and curly or kept long but upswept and held in place with encircling bands. This could not have been an easy style to wear for any but the youngest and slenderest women. However, from about 1810, practicality began to return with medium-weight fabrics, a wider choice of colours and prints, and more ornamentation at bodice, sleeve and hem. The basic column shape remained, but there was some scope for self-expression. Spencers (long-sleeved jackets stopping beneath the bust), pelisses (much the same but reaching three-quarters-way down the skirt) and bonnets all gave variety, not to mention warmth and comfort, to the outfit. It is this more wearable and elegant style of dress with which we people Jane Austen's world in our imaginations, reinforced by countless television adaptations, and justified certainly in the case of the three "Chawton" novels, arguably also in the others which were revised by her after 1809.

Male dress

During the same span of time male costume underwent a similar transformation, from the richly coloured brocaded suits of coat, waistcoat and knee breeches, topped off with a powdered wig, current in Jane Austen's youth, to the more sober and practical outfits of the Regency period. Knee breeches, stockings and buckled shoes gave place to light-coloured pantaloons (rather like the female leggings of today) tucked into high riding boots. Coats became plain and dark in colour, cut away in front to facilitate horsemanship, and revealing an abundance of white linen. Hair was worn short and unpowdered. These changes suited the lifestyle of the country gentleman. And it is no exaggeration to say that every English man above a certain rank, even if he spent most of his time in town, aspired to the ideal of the country gentleman, with all its connotations of independence, culture and dignity. The French court, arbiter of earlier eighteenth century fashions, had been discredited; in clothes as in so many other facets of life, English taste asserted its own pre-eminence.

CARTOON SHOWING A DANDY, 1812.

CHAPTER FIVE

The Immortal Jane Austen

ONE EVENING IN SEPTEMBER 1995, nine million people in the United Kingdom sat down to watch *Pride and Prejudice* on television. It is astonishing to think that nine million represents the entire population of England and Wales in Jane Austen's lifetime, only a small percentage of whom would have been literate. Following the BBC transmission, and with Emma Thompson's *Sense and Sensibility* adding to public awareness, the number of visitors to the Jane Austen museum at Chawton reached four hundred per day. More people are discovering the pleasures of Jane Austen all the time. She has the unique ability to appeal on many levels. Readers have attested that they seem to know Jane Austen's people better than the people in their own lives. This power is all the more remarkable considering the passage of time and transformation of manners.

It is an aspect of her genius that she never repeats a character, minor or major. Though each of her heroines is completely different from the others, she understands and sympathizes with the workings of all their hearts. These complex and fully-realized young women lend their individuality to the novels that contain them. Though related by the ironic vision, moral values, controlling intelligence and precision of language of their author, the world of each novel is a distinctive one, which we enter with a frisson of delight.

In each novel Jane Austen attempts something new, tackles new themes and responds to the changing social and cultural conditions of the world around her. She is perceptive and she is also funny. People laugh out loud at her books; and they come back to them time and time again. If these were merely novels of courtship, concerned with a small privileged section of society, they would hardly bear repeated readings. But so subtly does she load her narratives with meaning, they support not only a lifetime's fascination in many individuals, but a burgeoning academic industry.

Each generation is impelled to interpret her afresh in works of biography and literary criticism, taking every approach from popular to esoteric. Her works have reached massive new audiences through cinema, television and theatre adaptations. Sequels to her novels are being produced with dizzying frequency by modern authors whose imaginations engage with her own. Societies exist to honour her; she is everywhere, from classrooms to holiday itineraries. Interest is by no means confined to the English-speaking world. Even in her lifetime or shortly after, her novels were translated into French, and the twentieth century has seen translations into more than two dozen languages, from Finnish to Portuguese, from Romanian to Chinese. The novels have a particularly avid following in Japan, and a significant proportion of visitors to the Jane Austen museum at Chawton are Japanese. Jane Austen is surely unique in the devotion which she inspires in generation after generation of readers. This devotion shows no sign of diminishing as we move further in time from the culture and background of her novels; rather it is increasing with the years. No other writer is at once so sincerely loved and intimately known by the general public, and so well-respected and researched in academic circles.

Sense and Sensibility

THE INTEGRITY OF THE SELF and the claims of society lie at the heart of this novel, which explores the destiny of two sisters, Elinor and Marianne Dashwood. The world of *Sense and Sensibility* is a particularly public one. Much of life is lived communally; the heroines are forced into a great deal of empty socializing and their romantic and financial circumstances are the subject of speculation and curiosity. With the exception of their mother and the men they eventually marry, the characters surrounding the heroines are mean-spirited, impertinent or vulgar.

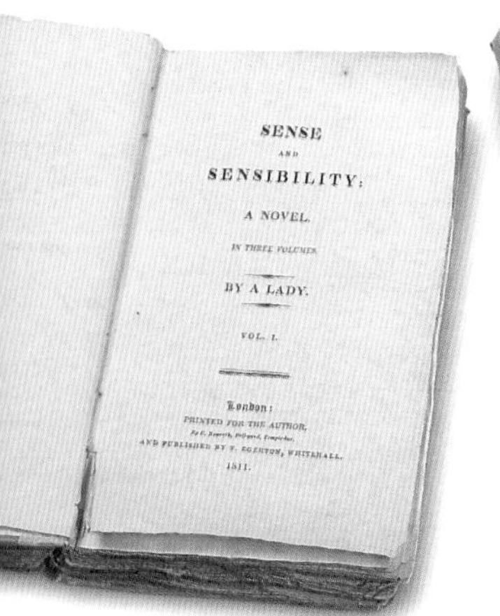

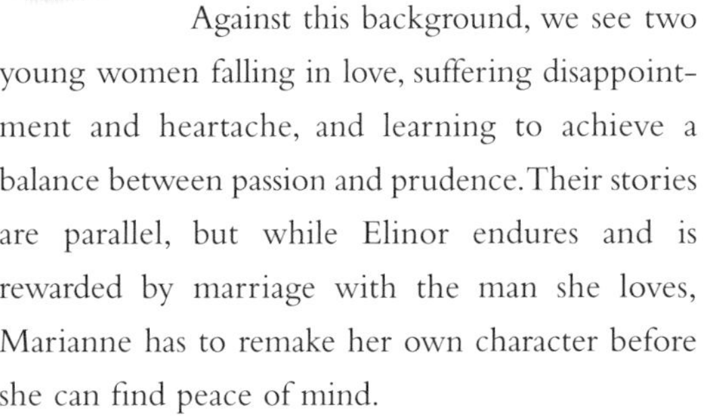

FIRST EDITION OF "SENSE AND SENSIBILITY", PUBLISHED 1811.

Against this background, we see two young women falling in love, suffering disappointment and heartache, and learning to achieve a balance between passion and prudence. Their stories are parallel, but while Elinor endures and is rewarded by marriage with the man she loves, Marianne has to remake her own character before she can find peace of mind.

The cult of sensibility

The earliest of her novels, *Sense and Sensibility* is a reaction to Jane Austen's youthful reading. The cult of sensibility, which was prevalent in the literature of that time, argued that to have overpowering feelings was a sign of superior character. It followed that it was as wrong as it was hopeless to try to control or hide such feelings, whatever inconvenience or suffering they may cause their owner or anybody else. Jane Austen had two quarrels with the cult of sensibility. The first was that people might exaggerate and falsify their feelings in order to be thought superior. The other was that even when feelings were deeply held and true, they did not excuse their owner from observing the common decencies of social behaviour.

The Dashwood sisters

By showing us how two sisters handle their love relationships, Jane Austen sets out to demonstrate the dangers of excessive sensibility. To say that Elinor Dashwood stands for sense and her sister Marianne for sensibility is so put the case too baldly. Elinor is sensible and prudent, but she too has strong feelings. It is just that she keeps them to herself; feelings should be private things, she – and her author – believe. Marianne is not without sense, but it has been overridden by the almost morbid cultivation of her sensibility. She possesses genuinely strong feelings, which she feeds and glories in, whether joy or grief. The conventions of society are beneath her notice, because she considers herself a superior person.

Most readers find Marianne's warmth of heart, spontaneity and openness of manners bewitching. They suit the spirit of our own age better than the stiff decorum she herself scorns. And Marianne's transgressions of society's rules hurt nobody more than herself, so there seems little to forgive her for. Most of the characters she is rude to are either too obtuse to notice – like the loveable but limited Mrs Jennings – or they are despicable anyway.

Nevertheless, such is Jane Austen's skill in manipulating our responses, we favour Elinor's point of view. We see most of the action of the novel through her eyes. Elinor, for all her calm good sense and self-control, is never insufferably priggish. We know that inwardly she suffers deeply, though the people around her have no idea. We understand that having a mother who can be as romantically unworldly as Marianne herself, almost foists on Elinor the role of the prudent one of the family. Elinor is finally saved from priggishness by her ability to laugh wryly at herself. Consider this passage, which follows Mrs Jennings' attempts to soothe Marianne's broken heart with a glass of the wine which her husband used to take for his gout:

> *"Dear Ma'am," replied Elinor, smiling at the difference of the complaints for which it was recommended, "how good you are! But I have just left Marianne in bed, and, I hope, almost asleep; and as I think nothing will be of so much service to her as rest, if you will give me leave, I will drink the wine myself." Mrs Jennings, though regretting that she had not been five minutes earlier, was satisfied with the compromise; and Elinor, as she swallowed the chief of it, reflected that, though its good effects on a cholicky gout were, at present, of little importance to her, its healing powers on a disappointed heart might be as reasonably tried on herself as on her sister.*

Marriage and society

One of the lessons that Marianne has to learn is that a nosy, vulgar character like Mrs Jennings may actually possess genuine warmth of heart, and be entitled to her respect and affection for that reason. But on the whole, the Dashwoods are not required to reassess their opinions of other people. Their task is rather to preserve, and if possible spread, the values which make them superior to the mercenary society all around. From the beginning of the novel, the Dashwood household has been characterized by affection, intelligence and integrity.

But while it remains a household of poor women it has no power to influence the larger social scene – rather, it is swamped by it. Only by marriage to like-minded men, Edward Ferrars and Colonel Brandon, can Elinor and Marianne become influential members of a local community and find fulfilment not only as individuals but as social beings.

THE THREE DASHWOOD SISTERS AND THEIR MOTHER.

Pride and Prejudice

FROM ITS FAMOUS first sentence to its almost fairytale ending, *Pride and Prejudice* sparkles with wit and youthful high spirits. The heroine is perhaps the most delightful of any created by Jane Austen – or by any other writer, for that matter. The dialogue is masterly, the comic characters wonderfully ridiculous and the plot has a most satisfying shape. If the novel lacks the depth of Jane Austen's later creations, it is unequalled in surface brilliance and humour.

The tone of the novel is a happy one. The heroine, Elizabeth Bennet, laughs at most of the follies around her, and we laugh with her. She has her share of suffering, but not enough to occupy a very large proportion of the narrative. Except for occasional moments of despair, her outlook is an optimistic one. Perhaps more optimistic than her economic circumstances warrant – for the Bennet girls really will be homeless when their father dies, and Mrs Bennet, for all her faults, should be given some credit for worrying about their future. Elizabeth's insouciance is partly the result of her nature, partly a reaction to her mother's fussing, but it is also an unconscious product of the author's youth. At the time she wrote *Pride and Prejudice*, Jane Austen had not failed to observe that in society as it stood, marriage was "the only honourable provision for well-educated young women of small fortune"; but she had hardly yet begun to reflect seriously on the predicament of dependent or dispossessed women.

I must confess that I think her as delightful a creature as ever appeared in print, and how I shall be able to tolerate those who do not like her at least I do not know.

JANE AUSTEN ON ELIZABETH BENNET

Elizabeth and Darcy

On the alternate advance and retreat between the hero and heroine of this novel, its interest, suspense and ultimate satisfaction depend. Their movements toward and away from one another have a dance-like quality. It has been said that with this novel Jane Austen hit upon the archetypal romantic plot, much used in our own day by formula writers. Independent-minded woman meets arrogant man and conceives an instant loathing for him. He is attracted, but resists acknowledging the fact even to himself. But he can't help thinking about her and eventually he demonstrates, by some act of exceptional tenderness and unselfishness, that for all his strength and self-sufficiency, he is enslaved by her charm. It is a potent story, which Jane Austen tells with intelligence and wit no other author comes near.

In such a plot, the heroine and hero are called on to bear considerable weight. They must be sufficiently complex and capable of change to engage our interest and make the vacillations between them convincing and not artificially drawn out. Their eventual coming together must seem as absolutely right as it once seemed totally unlikely.

The success of *Pride and Prejudice* is in large measure the success of Elizabeth Bennet and Mr Darcy as creations. And yet they are presented very differently, one from the inside, the other on the periphery of our vision. Darcy remains something of a wish-fulfilment figure, handsome and aloof. But that is entirely appropriate for this kind of romance. That Darcy is difficult for anybody to know, including ourselves, only heightens his appeal for the one woman whom he allows to glimpse his vulnerability beneath the social mask.

Elizabeth Bennet becomes known to us much more fully. It is impossible not to care about her destiny. She has a high opinion of herself and will neither sell herself short to a suitor like Mr Collins, nor allow a more socially powerful figure like Lady Catherine to get the better of her. But she will admit herself to be in the wrong when convinced by Mr Darcy's letter that she has been "blind, partial, prejudiced, absurd". With all her joyous spirits, Elizabeth has a serious side to her nature, for she is very deeply concerned to live a good and moral life. We love Elizabeth not only because she laughs, but because she thinks, grows and changes.

Light and bright and sparkling

After the charm of Elizabeth Bennet, *Pride and Prejudice* is loved for its gallery of comic characters. Mr and Mrs Bennet, Mr Collins and Lady Catherine de Bourgh are richly idiosyncratic creations who have achieved the status of classics; even those who have not read the novel are often familiar with their names, and Mr Collins has even given his to a particular kind of thank-you letter.

Mr Collins and Lady Catherine come as a package, as it were, for it is his ridiculous eulogies of his patroness that convict Mr Collins out of his own mouth during his first visit to Longbourn. His proposal to Elizabeth is one of the most richly comic scenes in English literature, especially prefaced as it is by his changing his choice from Jane to Elizabeth in the time it takes for Mrs Bennet to stir the fire. Later, when Elizabeth visits Hunsford, she has a chance to observe Mr Collins in obsequious attendance on Lady Catherine herself.

MRS BENNET BEING EMBARRASSING IN COMPANY.

Mrs Bennet is certainly no object of humour to Elizabeth, who is either embarrassed or ashamed of her mother. The "follies and nonsense, whims and inconsistencies," which amuse Elizabeth in her neighbours are no laughing matter so close to home. The humour mainly arises when Mr and Mrs Bennet are together, for she is so slow-witted that she no idea when he is mocking her. His sarcasm masquerades as politeness.

When she first read the novel in print, Jane Austen wondered whether it was perhaps "too light and bright and sparkling". The verbal wit of Mr Bennet and, less cruelly, of Elizabeth, certainly endow the novel with its special brilliance – but it is doubtful if any reader has ever complained of their excess.

THE WEDDING OF ELIZABETH AND DARCY.

Northanger Abbey

IN NORTHANGER ABBEY, we have two kinds of novels cleverly and most effectively welded into one. The Bath scenes which occupy the first part of the novel belong to the genre that describes a young lady's entrance into the world. The later chapters set in Northanger Abbey are a skit on the popular Gothic novels of the day.

With such literary origins, it is not surprising to find in *Northanger Abbey* a highly self-conscious work of art. Quite deliberately, Jane Austen keeps reminding us that we are reading a novel. This is appropriate in a work whose chief theme is the difference between illusion and reality, and the importance of knowing which we are dealing with at any one time.

The novel follows Catherine Morland's progress from innocence and delusion to understanding and clear sight. She never loses her honesty and unaffectedness, which is what makes her an attractive heroine despite being neither clever nor witty. But she does learn a few lessons in the ways of the world, while artlessly working her way into the affections of the hero. He is clever and witty – in fact, in his scrupulousness about language and ironic vision, Henry Tilney has often been thought to resemble Jane Austen herself.

ADLESTROP HOUSE, REFASHIONED IN GOTHIC STYLE.

A young lady's entrance into the world

This, the subtitle of Fanny Burney's highly successful *Evelina*, was a fruitful genre for female writing. An inexperienced girl who has grown up in the country is introduced into the social world of London or Bath, with all the novelties of experience and variety of characters that can be imagined. To preserve her reputation and attract the right kind of man to be her husband, she has to learn to read character in the odd people she encounters, some of whom may have designs upon her person or her money.

Jane Austen takes this convention, makes what use of it she pleases, and subverts what she finds far-fetched. Catherine Morland goes to Bath, all wide-eyed innocence, and encounters many novelties. But she does not set the town on fire with her beauty, as a real heroine would. One of the conventions of the genre was that the heroine's chaperone would add to her problems by embarrassing her in company or compromising her good name. Catherine's chaperone does neither – she is merely ineffectual. Mrs Allen belongs to that class of females who can raise no stronger emotion than surprise that any man should like them well enough to marry them. She fails Catherine in nothing more serious than omitting to tell her that she should not drive in an open carriage with a young man.

And so it goes on. The misunderstandings which are part of every heroine's experience are in Catherine's case very mild and everyday ones. Jane Austen shows us that the incidents of real life, while far removed from the wild happenings in novels, are actually just as important to the happiness of the individual – and just as interesting, if not more so, to read about.

Gothic horrors

Jane Austen's earliest writing had been in the form of burlesque, that is, making fun of a literary convention by exaggerating or flattening its features. The adventures that befall Catherine at Northanger, always ending in bathos, are a burlesque on the Gothic novel tradition.

Gothic novels were usually set in castles and abbeys in mountainous regions like Italy or the South of France, and involve the heroine discovering dark deeds. These are what Catherine Morland calls "horrid" novels – the equivalent of our horror films. She reads them for the pleasure of being frightened, and her imagination is so filled by them that she begins to regard them as a true representation of real life.

At Northanger Abbey she fancies all kinds of horrors and is disabused either by her own discovery of reality, or by Henry Tilney's putting her right. This is highly comic, but the finishing irony is that something unpleasant does happen to her, albeit of a most mundane nature.

Defence of the novel

Northanger Abbey contains Jane Austen's famous defence of the novelist's art. Catherine Morland's favourite reading is novels. "Yes, novels," Jane Austen writes, for "if the heroine of one novel be not patronized by the heroine of another, from whom can she expect protection and regard?" She gives a specimen of the common cant:

> *"And what are you reading Miss—?" "Oh, it is only a novel!" replies the young lady, while she lays down her book with affected indifference or momentary shame.—"It is only Cecilia or Camilla or Belinda"; or, in short, only some work in which the greatest powers of the mind are displayed, in which the most thorough knowledge of human nature, the happiest delineation of its varieties, the liveliest effusions of wit and humour, are conveyed to the world in the best-chosen language.*

It is a nice irony that though dangerous when confused with real life, novels can actually give us knowledge of our fellow human beings that surpasses that of real life.

ABOVE: CATHERINE MORLAND IN BATH. BELOW: "PERSUASION" AND "NORTHANGER ABBEY" WERE PUBLISHED IN 1818.

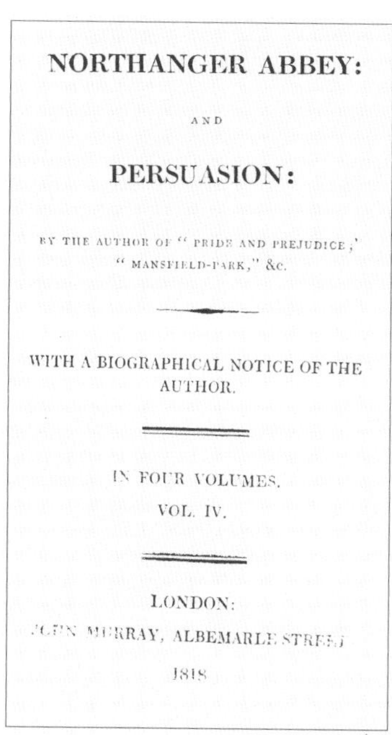

NORTHANGER ABBEY:

AND

PERSUASION:

BY THE AUTHOR OF "PRIDE AND PREJUDICE," "MANSFIELD-PARK," &c.

WITH A BIOGRAPHICAL NOTICE OF THE AUTHOR.

IN FOUR VOLUMES.

VOL. IV.

LONDON:

JOHN MURRAY, ALBEMARLE STREET.

1818.

Mansfield Park

FANNY PRICE AND EDMUND BERTRAM.

THE FIRST OF JANE AUSTEN'S novels to have been conceived and wholly written at Chawton, *Mansfield Park* is very different in tone from its predecessors. For some readers it is the most substantial and satisfying of Jane Austen's novels. Others like it the least, perhaps because wit and humour, though not absent from the novel, seem to be regarded with some suspicion.

Most controversial of all is the heroine, Fanny Price. Some feel as tenderly toward her as her author does; others find her too solemn. Fanny comes to Mansfield at the age of ten, a poor relation. Timid and self-effacing, she stands on the sidelines for the first half of the novel, observing the courtships and flirtations of her cousins the Bertrams and visitors to the neighbourhood, Henry and Mary Crawford.

The departure of some of these characters forces Fanny into a more prominent role in the second half of the novel. Now her own strength of character is tested by pressure to submit to the destiny chosen for her by the powerful men in her life. From being the most marginal figure in the Mansfield community, Fanny turns out to have its future welfare in her keeping.

Symbolism

Mansfield Park is exceptional among the novels for using the literary devices of symbolism and foreshadowing. They make a large contribution to the aesthetic qualities of the book. Three times Jane Austen brings these devices into play.

The first is the day out at Sotherton. The characters divide naturally into groups, which foreshadows their later involvement with one another. In the "wilderness" – itself symbolic – Fanny is forgotten while Edmund and Mary wander off together. Maria Bertram, accompanied by the man she is engaged to, Mr Rushworth, and the man she loves, Henry Crawford, arrives at a locked iron gate leading to a different part of the garden. Maria, metaphorically facing the prospect of marriage, has a feeling of constraint. While Mr Rushworth goes off to fetch the key, Maria allows Henry Crawford to help her scramble round the side of the gate and walk off toward a knoll in the distance – just as he will lead her into adultery later in the novel.

The next major event in the young people's lives is their absorption in amateur theatricals. Rehearsals allow them to rehearse the parts they would like to play in real life with one another. Maria and Henry enjoy many rehearsals of the scene in which they have to embrace as mother and long-lost son; while Mary's character has to declare her love for Edmund's, and boldly propose marriage. The fit between the characters in the novel, and those in the play, Mrs Inchbald's melodrama *Lovers' Vows*, is remarkable.

The third use of symbolism concerns William's cross. Fanny's beloved sailor brother William sends her an amber cross as a gift, an incident copied from life, as Jane Austen's brother Charles sent topaz crosses to his sisters. To wear the cross at the ball, Fanny needs a chain. Mary gives her one of her own necklaces, but it turns out that Fanny has been tricked into accepting what is really the gift of Henry, her unwelcome suitor. Meanwhile Edmund, the man Fanny secretly loves, buys a simple gold chain for his cousin. When she comes to try them, Fanny finds that Henry's necklace won't go through the cross, but Edmund's chain will. The symbolism is obvious, but subtle.

Mansfield and Portsmouth

Most of the action of the novel takes place at Mansfield Park, the elegant and comfortable mansion of Fanny's rich relations, the Bertram family. Fanny has been transplanted here from her home in the back streets of Portsmouth. Lady Bertram and

"IN VAIN DID LADY BERTRAM SMILE AND MAKE HER SIT ON THE SOFA WITH HERSELF AND PUG."

Mrs Price are sisters, starting off with the same chances in life, whose marriages have brought them very different status and lifestyles. Fanny is initially delighted when her uncle suggests she might like to visit Portsmouth again, after being away eight years. But the reality of her parents' home soon makes her revise her opinion.

We feel with Fanny the tumult, noise, disorder, dirt and confinement of a working-class home. It is not only shortage of money, it is bad management that makes the Prices' house so uncomfortable.

> *Her eyes could only wander from the walls marked by her father's head, to the table cut and notched by her brothers, where stood the tea-board never thoroughly cleaned, the cups and saucers wiped in streaks, the milk a mixture of motes floating in thin blue, and the bread and butter growing every minute more greasy than even Rebecca's hands had produced it. Her father read the paper, while her mother lamented over the ragged carpet as usual …*

Jane Austen paints her Portsmouth scenes convincingly. To be able to move comfortably from descriptions of country house life to such scenes of domestic squalor demonstrates a range for which she is not always given the credit she deserves.

Emma

"A HEROINE WHOM no-one but myself will much like," Jane Austen called her eponymous heroine when she was writing *Emma*. But readers do like Emma, very much, despite her faults of snobbery and vanity. She is an affectionate and patient daughter, a delightful aunt, and a loving friend to Mrs Weston. But it is the play of her mind that perhaps entrances us most.

Emma is often playful. It is one of the qualities which Mr Knightley loves her for, and which seems to promise them a happy partnership. But she can also be rational. We are told early in the novel that though she dearly loves her father, he is no companion to her. "He could not meet her in conversation, either rational or playful." Mr Knightley can. They are both natural leaders of their society, and function well together, long before they have recognized their mutual love. Consider this exchange, early in the novel, when a sudden fall of snow has produced panic in all the rest of the company:

While the others were variously urging and recommending, Mr Knightley and Emma settled it in a few brief sentences, thus –

> *"Your father will not be easy; why do not you go?"*
> *"I am ready, if the others are."*
> *"Shall I ring the bell?"*
> *"Yes, do."*
> *And the bell was rung, and the carriages spoken for.*

Emma dominates her novel to an extent not equalled by any other Jane Austen heroine, and it is rightly named after her. While most of the novels begin by explaining the family circumstances before coming in to focus on the heroine, the first words of this novel are: "Emma Woodhouse", and the first sentence is a description of her personality: "handsome, clever and rich, with a comfortable home and a happy disposition."

EMMA WOODHOUSE WHO DOMINATES THE NOVEL NAMED AFTER HER.

All Jane Austen's narratives are seen through a young woman's eyes, but Emma Woodhouse does not just experience, she shapes events. Rich and powerful within her home and her community – a rare state for an unmarried woman – she enjoys exceptional freedom of action. Other heroines are called on to react to what happens about them; Emma is, by contrast, proactive. Because there are relatively few external constraints on her behaviour, she has all the more scope to make mistakes: some comic, some seriously affecting other people's lives, some seeming to jeopardize her own happiness. The catalogue of Emma's mistakes gives most of the impetus and interest to the story.

A detective story

The novelist P.D. James has called *Emma* a great detective story, and it has claims to be the first of that genre. Not, of course, the kind of detective story that revolves around murders, police detectives and amateur sleuths. But the novel certainly has at its heart a secret,which is hidden until nearly the end from both the central consciousness – Emma – and the reader.

Almost no first-time reader of the novel even guesses that there is a secret, much less what it is. But the pleasure is by no means diminished on a second or subsequent reading; if anything it is enhanced. Now the enjoyment lies in picking up the clues and being amused by Emma's obliviousness to what is going on under her nose. The clues are all there, so well hidden by Jane Austen that they make no impression before the secret is known, and yet so precise that we cannot accuse her of leading us astray.

Our first reading brings home to us directly the very lesson Emma herself has to learn, namely how difficult it is to interpret other people's behaviour. Subsequent readings of the novel have an added intellectual dimension in appreciation of Jane Austen's artistry.

A sense of community

Emma is unusual among the novels in focusing on the heroine as a member of a community. Other heroines will achieve this position with marriage, beyond the span of the book; Emma has it already, and her marriage will only confirm and perhaps enlarge her sphere of influence. So while the other narratives follow their heroines away from home on a variety of learning experiences, *Emma* is static. The action takes place wholly in Highbury, the "large and populous village, almost amounting to a town" where Emma has lived all her life.

EMMA WITH MR KNIGHTLEY IN ANOTHER ADAPTATION OF THE NOVEL.

In another departure from Jane Austen's usual practice, *Emma* embraces different levels of society. Speaking parts are confined, as usual, to members of the gentry, but other classes have a physical presence; individuals are named and differentiated, their various doings acknowledged. The impression is gradually built up of a thriving, busy community. We hear of shopkeepers, schoolteachers, lawyers, a physician, an innkeeper, an ostler, a bailiff, a tenant farmer and servants from the various households, as well as the family of a sick cottager visited by Emma.

All these people, to a greater or lesser extent, are subject to the patronage and goodwill of Emma Woodhouse. She has been placed by her creator in a more comfortable and privileged position than any other of the heroines, and the lesson she must learn in the course of the novel is how to fulfil the duties it entails. In one sense the community exists to test Emma; this is a novel about village life because Emma's particular character demands this particular trial. In another sense, of course, the community has a life and reality of its own, and Emma over-estimates her importance to it. That is another lesson that this heroine, "faultless in spite of all her faults" as Mr Knightley thinks of her, has to learn.

Persuasion

JANE AUSTEN WAS ABOUT forty years old when she wrote *Persuasion*. Until then, she had always taken as her heroine a young woman at the thresh-hold of life, inexperienced, falling in love for the first time, aged somewhere between seventeen and twenty-one. Now she told a different kind of story. Anne Elliot is twenty-seven, with a fully mature mind. For her, falling in love is something that belongs to her past. Eight years before the novel opens, she had become engaged to marry Captain Wentworth of the Royal Navy, but was persuaded to break off the engagement for reasons of prudence. She has spent the last eight years regretting the decision, and does not expect to find love again.

LYME REGIS IN 1810.

The novel has two settings. From Michaelmas to Christmas Anne resides in the Somerset countryside, first at the home of her married sister, then with her friend Lady Russell. Two days are spent by the sea at Lyme, where events occur that will change the destiny of several of the characters. After Christmas Anne goes reluctantly to live in Bath. Her spend-thrift, snobbish father, Sir Walter Elliot, has taken a house here in order to economize, while his country estate is let to Captain Wentworth's sister and her husband, Admiral Croft. Anne experiences Bath as a place of confinement, artificiality and useless-ness. She is rescued from it by Captain Wentworth's gradual realization that he is still in love with her, as she has never ceased to be in love with him.

Persuasion is one of the most tender love stories ever written, and Anne's gentle, patient but firm character makes her a fitting heroine for Jane Austen's most mature novel. "Almost too good for me," Jane Austen called her. Could she be modelled on Cassandra, whose reserved nature she seems to share, and whose heart seems to have remained similarly faithful to her lost love? If so, she is Jane's tribute to the sister she had admired all her life, and perhaps her attempt to make that sister's modestly concealed virtues understood by the world.

An autumnal story

"The influence so sweet and so sad of the autumnal months in the country," permeates this novel, both literally and metaphorically. When Anne accompanies the others on a country walk, her object is not to be in the way of anybody:

> *Her pleasure in the walk must arise from the exercise and the day, from the view of the last smiles of the year upon the tawny leaves and withered hedges, and from repeating to herself some few of the thousand poetical descriptions extant of autumn, that season of peculiar and inexhaustible influence on the mind of taste and tenderness . . .*

In such passages it is possible to feel Jane Austen coming under the influence of the romantic movement in poetry, allowing herself a personal response to nature that is new in her fiction. Rather like Anne Elliot herself, it could be said that Jane Austen erred on the side of prudence in her youth, and learned romance as she grew older. Later in the same passage, on hearing Captain Wentworth speak with enthusiasm to Louisa Musgrove,

> *Anne could not immediately fall into a quotation again. The sweet scenes of autumn were for a while put by, unless some tender sonnet, fraught with the apt analogy of the declining year, with declining happiness, and the images of youth, and hope, and spring, all gone together, blessed her memory.*

Though young by today's standards, Anne feels she is in the autumn of her life. Her "bloom" is gone, and she is no longer regarded as one of the marriageable young ladies in company. The older women accept her as one of themselves. This is partly because she is so sensible, but also because sadness and regret have made her seem old before her time. Knowing herself loved, by the end of the novel, will give her a new spring of youth and beauty.

Fine naval fervour

In *Persuasion* Jane Austen contrasts three sets of characters, and questions which set is most fit to have the leadership of the country in their hands. There are the people of high birth like the Elliots and Dalrymples, who live empty, useless lives, who are inhospitable and snobbish, and over-concerned with appearances. By losing Kellynch through his own extravagance, Sir Walter shows that local communities can no longer rely on the traditonal landed gentry for leadership. They are becoming effete. Then there are the old-fashioned Musgroves, "not much educated, and not at all elegant," but hospitable and unpretentious. This type is dying out, however – even their own children have "more modern minds and manners". Anne greatly prefers the Musgroves to her own relations, for their genuine warmth of heart, but they are not capable of leading the country into the modern age, and their children are lightweight. There is another set of people even more to Anne's taste: the naval families. Their vigour, bravery, friendliness and loyalty to one another she finds bewitching. "Only they know how to live," she believes. The novel ends with Anne glorying in being a sailor's wife, and with Jane Austen praising the profession for both its "domestic virtues" and "national importance".

MANUSCRIPT OF THE CANCELLED CHAPTER 10.

ANNE ELLIOT AND CAPTAIN WENTWORTH.

Memoirs and Biographies

AT THE TIME OF HER DEATH, Jane Austen had two completed manuscripts not yet published, *Northanger Abbey* and *Persuasion*. Her brother Henry superintended their publication together in four volumes, with a preface written by himself, which he called *A Biographical Notice of the Author*.

The Biographical Notice

Always more desirous of fame for his sister than she had been herself, Henry had divulged the secret of her authorship on more than one occasion, somewhat to her distress. Now he actually printed her name, gave a very brief outline of her life, and a fuller description of her manners, accomplishments, reading, tastes and character.

"When the public," he begins, "which has not been insensible to the merits of *Sense and Sensibility*, *Pride and Prejudice*, *Mansfield Park*, and *Emma*, shall be informed that the hand which guided that pen is now mouldering in the grave, perhaps a brief account of Jane Austen will be read with a kindlier sentiment than simple curiosity." It was the first appearance of the words "Jane Austen" in print.

IN THIS HOUSE JANE AUSTEN LIVED HER LAST DAYS AND DIED 18 TH. JULY 1817

MEMORIAL PLAQUE ON THE WINCHESTER HOUSE WHERE JANE AUSTEN DIED.

Henry writes with touching brotherly pride, but his portrait of the author is an insufferably pious one. He presents her as the perfect lady, shrinking from publication, unmotivated by money, deprecating low morals in literature, graceful and sweet in her demeanour, ladylike in her occupations and accomplishments. He rather improbably claims that she would find refuge in silence rather than utter a severe expression about anyone, and ends by saying that her opinions "accorded strictly with those of our Established Church".

One cannot help but feel that if Jane herself had read this, her reaction would have been, as she once wrote of a too-good heroine, "Pictures of perfection make me sick and wicked". Though it is impossible these days to read Henry's *Notice* without detecting its hidden agenda, it successfully established an image of Jane Austen that long prevailed, and which is still not without its potency.

The Memoir

Nothing more was written about Jane Austen's life or character for fifty years. Meanwhile, apart from a brief period in the 1820s, her novels remained constantly in print and attracted a small but devoted readership in each generation. In the late 1860s it occurred to her nephew James Edward Austen-Leigh that the public was ready for a fuller account than provided by his uncle Henry, and that his own recollections, and those of his sisters and cousins, should be gathered and preserved before it was too late. The result was the *Memoir of Jane Austen* of 1869.

The great charm of this book is Austen-Leigh's evocation of a vanished age from the standpoint of Victorian "progress". He writes affectionately but with some astonishment of the simple, homely life lived by his relations in the eighteenth century.

He was a young man of nineteen when his aunt died, not old enough to assess her personality disinterestedly. But he knew her sister, brothers and even her mother in his maturity. He had grown up in the same childhood home – Steventon Rectory – and had visited her at Southampton and Chawton. Of Steventon he writes with a personal affection:

> *This was the cradle of her genius. These were the first objectswhich inspired her young heart with a sense of the beauties of nature. In strolls along those wood-walks, thick-coming fancies rose in her mind, and gradually assumed the forms in which they came forth into the world.In that simple church she brought them all into subjectionto the piety which ruled her life and supported her in death.*

It was no part of Austen-Leigh's brief to amend the image of Jane Austen as a proper Christian lady, contented with her lot – like Henry, James Edward was a clergyman, and a Victorian to boot. But the happy portrait that emerges is a beguiling one, and supplies many details of Austen family life that must otherwise have been lost.

Twentieth-century biography

The scene becomes crowded in the present century. In 1913 two later members of the Austen-Leigh line published *Jane Austen: Her Life and Letters, a Family Record*, which was updated and expanded with much new material by Deirdre le Faye and published by the British Museum Press in 1989, a substantial and scholarly account of the life from which speculation and imaginative insight have been quite deliberately excluded. Le Faye is also the editor of the most recent edition of *Jane Austen's Letters*, first published in 1932 with a wealth of fascinating notes by R.W. Chapman.

In 1938 appeared the first full study of the subject generated outside the family in *Jane Austen: A Biography* by Elizabeth Jenkins. A highly readable portrait of the life and times, it remained the standard work for forty years or more. In many ways – psychological insight, feeling for eighteenth century culture, flowing prose – it has still not yet been surpassed.

ELIZABETH AUSTEN, JANE'S SISTER-IN-LAW, DISLIKED BY HER ACCORDING TO ONE BIOGRAPHER. THERE IS LITTLE EVIDENCE FOR SUCH A VIEW.

Nowadays the biographies come thick and fast, with a variety of approaches. Some focus on a particular aspect such as my own *Jane Austen's England* and *Jane Austen's Family Through Five Generations*. Some seek a bête-noir in one or other family member and build up their Jane Austen round that. Some discover a Jane Austen at odds with her society, or one with something of a split personality, like Jane Aiken Hodge's thoughtful *Double Life of Jane Austen*. Amid much that is trivial, innacurate or derivative, some books stand out. Jan Fergus's *Jane Austen,* for example, in the Macmillan Literary Life series, most refreshingly and informatively focuses on the author's professional life.

Serious works by respected biographers David Nokes and Claire Tomalin are forthcoming. Every age has the right and the need to reinterpret the great figures of the past in the light of its own understanding and concerns.

The Critics

CONTEMPORARY CRITICAL NOTICE concentrated on the morality, rather than the artistry, of Jane Austen's work. In a review of *Sense and Sensibility* shortly after its publication in 1811, the *British Critic* assured its female readers that they would encounter "many sober and salutary maxims for the conduct of life". *The Critical Review* also praised the "excellent lesson" and "useful moral" of this "genteel, well-written" story.

The publication of *Emma* attracted a long and respectful article, which we know Jane Austen read with pleasure, in the *Quarterly Review*. Written by Sir Walter Scott, the review was the first to recognize that scenes of everyday life, perceptively handled, could furnish material for the highest art. The same journal, but a different reviewer, noticed the posthumously published *Northanger Abbey* and *Persuasion* in terms that reverted to the earlier approach. Miss Austen's novels may safely be recommended, he rather condescendingly wrote, "not only as among the most unexceptional of their class, but as combining, in an eminent degree, instruction with amusement."

The Victorians

Amid the great Victorian fictional bill of fare, Jane Austen was a minority taste; yet the critic George Henry Lewes could observe in 1859 that without ever having been highly popular, Jane Austen's novels had survived those of her more widely-read contemporaries, such as Maria Edgeworth and Fanny Burney, whose work was now outdated and forgotten. Lewes was Jane Austen's staunchest advocate in the Victorian era. Despite the emergence of so many giants of the novel, he still maintained that Jane Austen was "the greatest artist that has ever written, using the term to signify the most perfect mastery over the means to her end". He concluded:

> *The delight derived from her pictures arises from our sympathy with ordinary characters, our relish of humour, and our intellectual pleasure in art for art's sake ... Her fame, as we think, must endure. Such art as hers can never grow old, never be superseded. But, after all, miniatures are not frescoes, and her works are miniatures. Her place is among the Immortals; but the pedestal is erected in a quiet niche of the great temple.*

THE THREE VOLUMES OF "EMMA" SPECIALLY BOUND FOR THE PRINCE REGENT, TO WHOM THE NOVEL IS DEDICATED.

Among those whom Lewes introduced to Jane Austen's novels was Charlotte Brontë. However, she was not as impressed as he had expected. "The Passions are perfectly unknown to her," she wrote; "even to the Feelings she vouchsafes no more than an occasional graceful but distant recognition; too frequent converse with them would but ruffle the elegance of her progress." Charlotte Brontë had read only two of the novels, however, and encountered neither Marianne Dashwood's passion for Willoughby, nor Fanny Price's neglected heart, which would surely have appealed to her more than the self-confident wit of Elizabeth Bennet and Emma Woodhouse. "Jane Austen was a complete and most sensible lady, but a very incomplete and rather insensible (not senseless) woman," was Charlotte Brontë's verdict on a genius very different from her own.

The novelist Anthony Trollope presented the good-for-females-to-read argument in a particularly Victorian way, assuring his readers that Jane Austen's novels were "free from an idea or word that can pollute ... a sweet lesson of homely household womanly virtue is ever being taught."

As a woman, the novelist Mrs Oliphant was able to perceive different virtues: "a fine vein of feminine cynicism" and "stinging, yet soft-voiced contempt".

The twentieth century

Our own century began in a flurry of prettily illustrated editions and chatty "appreciation", culminating in the cult of the "Janeites", devotees of the novels – the word was coined by Kipling. Even Henry James, whose own fiction of psychological subtlety owes a great debt to Jane Austen, dismissed ideas that a woman could be a conscious artist, calling her novels merely "instinctive and charming". D.H. Lawrence reacted against this cosiness, calling her "thoroughly unpleasant, English in the bad, mean, snobbish sense of the word." The prettiness of her world, the narrowness of her range, and her concentration on woman's experience, together with the fact that the novels were amenable to being read purely for pleasure by "ordinary readers", combined to keep her out of the male world of scholarship and criticism developing in the universities in the first half of the century.

This position was breached by Mary Lascelles in her seminal *Jane Austen and her Art* of 1939. Nine years later the influential F.R. Leavis accorded her a place within "The Great Tradition" of the novel. Male academics started to take her seriously. Some of them began to find the work of this most ladylike of novelists angry rather than cosy. Phrases like "Regulated Hatred", "The Opposing Self" and "Irony as Defence and Discovery" entered the discourse.

Marilyn Butler first placed Jane Austen firmly in an historical context with her *Jane Austen and the War of Ideas* in 1975. In 1932 Rebecca West, in a preface to an edition of the novels, had claimed Jane Austen as a writer of "quite conscious feminism" applying "strong feeling and audacious thought" to a discussion of women's place in society. But the times were not right for such a claim to be attended to. The first full-length scholarly study to take this approach was Margaret Kirkham's *Jane Austen: Feminism and Fiction* of 1983.

Now it is impossible to write Jane Austen criticism without taking account of feminist and post-colonial thinking. Academics in universities worldwide are contributing to the present flood of critical books and articles on every conceivable facet of Jane Austen. For six novels to support such a body of work, is proof itself of their complexity and inexhaustibility for all ages.

CHARLOTTE BRONTË, A NOVELIST WHO FOUND JANE AUSTEN'S ART "SHREWD AND OBSERVANT" BUT LACKING IN POETRY.

Dramatizations

THE FIRST DRAMATIZATIONS of Jane Austen's novels were done for the stage. The earliest was the 1906 play of *Pride and Prejudice* by Mary K.M.MacKaye. *Pride and Prejudice*, with its abundance of witty dialogue which can be lifted straight from the page, its eloquent, spirited heroine and its highly comic minor characters, has always been the favoured novel for adaptation for either stage or screen. A version by Helen Jerome played in New York in 1935 and in London the following year. 1936 also saw the production of *Miss Elizabeth Bennet* by A.A. Milne. A product of its period – as all adaptations must be, albeit unconsciously – Milne's script, though relatively faithful to the plot, has something of the flavour of Noel Coward in its stylized and cynical repartee.

GREER GARSON AND LAURENCE OLIVIER IN THE REVILED 1940 FILM ADAPTATION OF "PRIDE AND PREJUDICE".

Film and musicals

Fascination with *Pride and Prejudice* continued unabated. It was made into a film in 1940, with Laurence Olivier as Darcy and Greer Garson as Elizabeth. Though one of the co-writers of the screenplay was Aldous Huxley, this is very much Hollywood's vision of quaint old England. It is significant that the film was made at the very moment when Britain was undergoing its "darkest hour". Whether the sub-text was to elicit support for an English tradition in jeopardy, or to suggest that the old country's greatness lay irretrievably in the past, this film, a travesty of the novel, certainly did no service to Jane Austen. Audiences of the film can have come away with no idea of the subtlety, profundity and timelessness of her art.

Two musicals based on *Pride and Prejudice* were produced after the war. In New York *First Impressions*, with Hermione Gingold as Mrs Bennet, ran for eighty-four performances in 1959. It was another attempt to render period England for an audience who had enjoyed *My Fair Lady*. Five years later a second version appeared in Johannesburg. Both musicals almost inevitably had the effect of trivializing a great work. Nevertheless, the fact that *Pride and Prejudice* was seen as source material for a modern popular art form is in itself testimony to Jane Austen's enduring appeal.

The modern period

Reflecting a steadily growing interest in Jane Austen, stage adaptations of all the novels have been made during the last few decades and have done the provincial rounds with varying degrees of mild success. But in terms of Jane Austen dramatizations, this period is really the preserve of the BBC. In the 1960s, 1970s and 1980s, the BBC Classic Serials department brought many great novels to the small screen, including all those of Jane Austen, some of them more than once. *Pride and Prejudice*, for example, was made in black and white in 1967, with Celia Bannerman as Elizabeth, and in colour in 1980, with Elizabeth Garvie in the main role, and a script by the novelist Fay Weldon.

Free from the commercial imperatives of other media, and backed by the resources – artistic as well as financial – of a great corporation, these productions are deservedly renowned for their writing, acting, design and direction. Respectful to the originals, with great attention paid to getting the visual details right, and many distinguished character actors involved, they were watched by huge audiences around the world. For all their good intentions, however, these

BBC versions have a tendency to look rather static, rather stilted, rather superficial. So bewitching is the physical world of Jane Austen when recreated for the screen, so pretty the dresses and so desirable the houses, that the deeper levels of meaning in the novels can hardly struggle through. The impression is apt to be given that these are novels about privileged young ladies with nothing better to do than look for husbands, lacking relevance for today.

Developments in the 1990s

This problem has been triumphantly overcome with the latest advance in rendering Jane Austen's novels for a modern mass audience. The breakthrough has been the use of film rather than video, whether commissioned for television or cinema showing. As Sue Birtwistle, producer of the 1995 version of *Pride and Prejudice* says of videotape, "I don't feel it serves drama well. It always looks undernourished; it's too present, too literal. Unpoetic, if you like. We wanted scenes to have a freedom that is just impossible to achieve recording on video in the studio."

In 1995 three productions – all of which were award winning – were shown, each of which exploited the potential of film. The first and most modestly budgeted was *Persuasion*, first transmitted on British television at Easter 1995, with subsequent cinema showings internationally. There is a naturalism about this production that makes the viewer feel what it would really be like to live in Jane Austen's time. Dresses are just dresses, not elaborately designed fashion plates; interiors are poorly lit at night. This restraint has the effect of foregrounding the emotions of the characters, making them real people with whom we can empathize. It is a lovely low-key production, admirably suited to the autumnal feel of the original.

Much more exuberant is the adaptation of *Pride and Prejudice* by Andrew Davies, shown later the same year. The sense of activity and expansiveness that the producer aimed for is certainly achieved, with some ravishing location shots. However, the temptation to concentrate on the glossy externals of Jane Austen's world at the expense of feeling is not wholly avoided.

GWYNETH PALTROW AND JEREMY NORTHAM IN THE 1996 CINEMA ADAPTATION OF "EMMA".

More impressive, in terms of doing justice to the humour and emotion of the author's creation, is the Columbia film of *Sense and Sensibility*, released in the United States in late 1995 and in Britain early in 1996. With a clever and witty screenplay by Emma Thompson, who also takes the role of Elinor, well supported by an array of splendid actors including Kate Winslet as a most moving Marianne, this film will be the benchmark against which future productions of Jane Austen novels will be measured. In 1996 two versions of *Emma* were produced – a Hollywood version starring Gwyneth Paltrow and a televison version, again scripted by Andrew Davies starring Kate Beckinsale as the eponymous heroine.

OSCAR WINNER EMMA THOMPSON WITH HUGH GRANT IN THE ACCLAIMED "SENSE AND SENSIBILITY".

Sequels and Completions

LOVERS, ONE MIGHT even say addicts, of Jane Austen – and we are legion – long more than anything for more of our favourite writer's work. Our greatest regret is that she lived only long enough to write six novels, and that she was at the height of her creative power when she died. Had she been granted a normal lifespan, she might have doubled her literary output, and written on even into the Victorian age.

A number of authors have attempted to assuage their own cravings, and satisfy those of other people, by completing the various unfinished fragments, or by writing sequels to the six novels. For some readers, these are the next best thing to Jane Austen herself. They offer further chances to inhabit her very special, recognizable world. Other readers find them disappointing, their prose dull and slack, their plots and incidents either mundane or far-fetched, and their characterization derivative. Whatever the view taken, the very multiplicity of these efforts, especially in recent years, and the fact that publishers find it worthwhile to publish them, indicate an insatiable appetite for Jane Austen not matched by any other classic author.

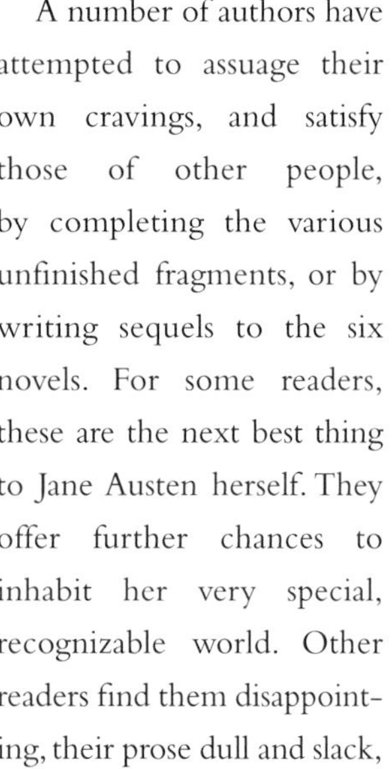

CATHERINE HUBBACK, NIECE OF JANE AUSTEN, WHO FIRST COMPLETED "THE WATSONS".

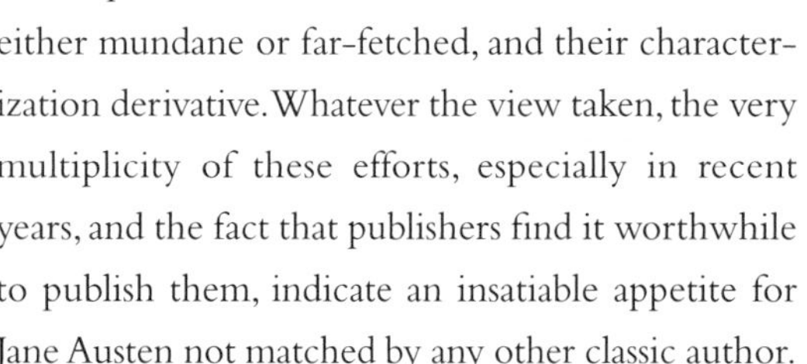

Completions

The Watsons was begun and abandoned during Jane Austen's residence in Bath. Her reasons for putting it aside might have been that she was too unsettled to write after her father's death, or that the situation of the heroine, poor and dispossessed, too closely resembled her own. When the story begins Emma Watson has lost the home and expectation of independence she enjoyed as her aunt's heiress, and has been returned to her impoverished family on the second marriage of that aunt. She returns to sisters whose hunt for a husband has become desperate, and to an ailing clergyman father whose imminent death will leave them all dependent on the charity of their narrow-minded brother.

Emma Watson is an attractive personality, refusing either to feel sorry for herself or to compromise her principles, and the opening chapters introduce a variety of other interesting characters, many of them despicable. It is unlikely therefore that Jane Austen abandoned the novel because she ran out of ideas for its development, but easy to see that the story might be too painful for her to continue in 1805.

The first completion of *The Watsons* was published in 1850 and the latest in 1996. Jane Austen's own niece Catherine Hubback began the whole business with a completion which she called *The Younger Sister*. The latest effort, Joan Aiken's *Emma Watson*, by telling the tale afresh from the beginning, avoids the "join" which completions always betray between Jane Austen's sparkling prose and the new material.

Sanditon also offers scope for finishing an intriguing story. It was begun by Jane Austen in January 1817 and laid aside in March when she could no longer hold a pencil. Extraordinarily, the twelve chapters she wrote betray no weakness of any kind. Inventive, even experimental, the writing explores new themes. A great deal of fun is had at the expense of hypochondriacs – a brave subject for a dying woman to tackle. The heroine, Charlotte Heywood, is a down-to-earth observer of other people's passions and follies, without her own heart seeming to be involved, and from the fragment it is not obvious who the hero is going to be.

There have been at least three continuations of *Sanditon*, one of which "by Jane Austen and Another Lady" in 1975 was particularly successful, and a film is in the pipeline.

Sequels

Even thicker on the ground than completions are sequels to the six novels. Unfortunately the ingenuity expended on the plots is rarely matched by sensitivity to the spirit of the originals.

Some take up the story at the point where the original ends. *Pemberley* by Emma Tennant shows us the Darcys in their first year of marriage – they have difficulty conceiving a child – while Rachel Billington's *Perfect Happiness*, which takes its title from the last sentence of *Emma*, questions the happy-ever-after convention of that ending. *Elinor and Marianne*, takes up the story of the Dashwood sisters and is also by Emma Tennant. This book finds a new twist to this approach by having the newly-married sisters writing letters to one another.

Another type of sequel takes the minor characters and asks what happened to them. Mrs Francis Brown was the first in this field with her *Margaret Dashwood* of 1929 and *Susan Price* of 1930, in which younger sisters have their chance to step into their elders' limelight. A later version of Susan Price's story is told in *Mansfield Revisited* by Joan Aiken, who has also made Jane Fairfax of *Emma* into the eponymous heroine of a novel.

Even more peripheral characters are sometimes brought to the fore. In *Miss Abigail's Part* by Judith Terry we see the world of Mansfield Park through the servants' eyes. *Mrs Goddard, Mistress of a School*, by family descendant Joan Austen-Leigh, is a recent epistolary novel, which cleverly tells a story concurrent with the action of *Emma*, the events of that novel impinging every now and again on Mrs Goddard's consciousness.

Sequel is hardly an adequate word for stories which deliberately and dizzyingly mix up characters from different novels. *Gambles and Gambols* by an author rather curiously known as 'Memoir' ends with the pairing off of Mary Crawford and Colonel Fitzwilliam; Kitty Bennet and James Morland; Isabella Thorpe and Tom Bertram; and Georgiana Darcy and William Price. Some authors – and readers – simply cannot have too much of a good thing.

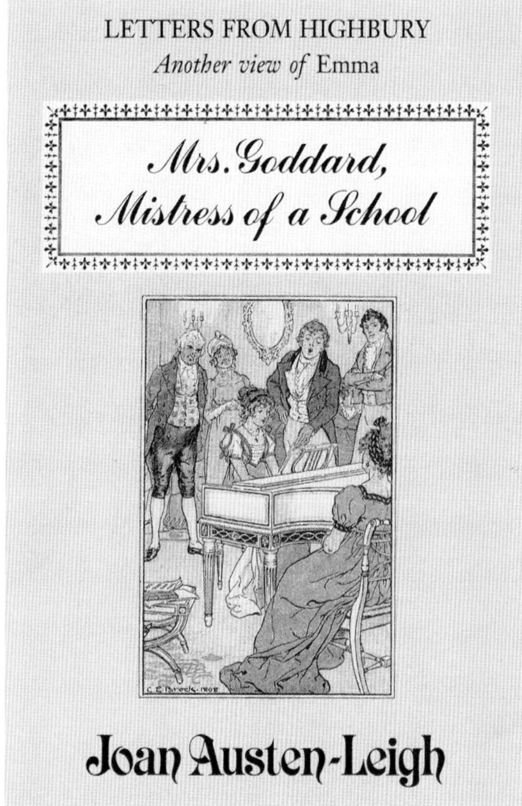

COVER OF ONE OF THE MOST RECENT JANE AUSTEN SEQUELS.

The Museum at Chawton

PLAQUE ON JANE AUSTEN'S HOUSE.

THE HOUSE IN WHICH Jane Austen lived for the last eight happy and productive years of her life is now a museum. Here visitors can see the rooms in which she lived and worked, items owned by herself and her family, contemporary costume and displays illustrating the events of her life. The garden, outbuildings and peaceful village setting complete the experience of stepping back into the secure and tranquil world that gave birth to the novels.

The history of the house

A substantial brick house built some time before 1712, it is now known officially as "Jane Austen's House", though to writers on Jane Austen it is usually Chawton Cottage. In early documents it carries the curious name "Petty Johns", but this had been dropped by the Austens' day. The property was conveyed to Thomas Knight in 1769 for £123. Shortly afterward it became an inn, known as the New Inn, but by 1791 it was again privately occupied. The tenant's death in 1808 enabled Edward Knight, who had meanwhile inherited the Chawton estate, to offer the cottage to his mother and sisters. He spent about £80 making it comfortable for them. He owned much of the property in the village, including of course Chawton Manor, which Jane Austen referred to as the Great House.

Of the other occupants of the cottage, Mrs Austen died in 1827, Martha Lloyd left to marry

THE HOUSE AT CHAWTON WHERE JANE AUSTEN LIVED FROM 1809 TO 1817.

Francis Austen as his second wife the following year, and Cassandra lived on until 1845. At the time of the 1841 census she was living in the cottage with three maids and one manservant; Henry Austen and his second wife Eleanor were staying with her. After Cassandra's death the cottage was divided into three dwellings for farm-workers' families.

It remained in this state until 1947, when it was bought for £3,000 from the Knight family by Mr T. Edward Carpenter in memory of his son, Lieutenant Philip Carpenter, who had been killed on active service in 1944. With some help from the Jane Austen Society and a public appeal Mr Carpenter repaired, endowed, and in 1949 opened the house as a museum, administered by the Jane Austen Memorial Trust. The present curator is Mr Carpenter's grandson.

Contents and displays

Many personal items which had been kept within the family have been returned to the museum. These include a lock of Jane Austen's hair, music books in her hand, several items of jewellery owned by her, including the topaz cross given by her brother Charles, and some delightful examples of her needlework, the most impressive of which is the large patchwork quilt hanging now in the bedroom that she shared with Cassandra.

Family possessions that have been bought or donated to the house over the years include numerous portraits, a Hepplewhite bureau-bookcase and chairs from Steventon Rectory, and Edward Knight's Wedgwood dinner service from Godmersham, which is displayed on the dining-room table. Nearby is a small table at which Jane Austen sometimes wrote, slipping her paper under a blotter when callers arrived. It is said that she asked for a squeaky door not to be oiled, as it gave her warning of anybody's approach.

In this room too is preserved the original fire grate and hob on which it was Jane Austen's duty to boil the copper kettle for breakfast. The cupboard in one of the alcoves would have contained supplies of tea, sugar and the household china. In the drawing room, the Clementi piano of 1810 is probably similar to the one bought by Jane Austen for the cottage.

Many original and facsimile letters and documents of the family are displayed in cases and on the walls.

There are sets of her books including a first edition of *Pride and Prejudice* owned by Lady Caroline Lamb. Displays showing the various houses lived in or visited by Jane Austen and illustrations from her books adorn the walls. One room containes memorabilia pertaining to the careers of her two naval brothers. There is an attractive display of costume from the period 1809 to 1845.

THE GREAT HOUSE AT CHAWTON.

Garden and courtyard

The garden, where visitors are welcome to picnic, is planted with many of the flowers and shrubs mentioned by Jane Austen in her letters, like sweet williams, columbines, mignonette, laburnum, lilac and philadelphus. In the outbuildings clustered round the courtyard can be seen the washtub and oven used by the Austens' servants, and most poignantly of all, the donkey carriage in which Jane Austen used to take air and exercise when she became too weak to walk.

A bookshop stocks all books by and about Jane Austen currently in print, together with audio and video versions, and a selection of second-hand and antiquarian books of interest to collectors.

Jane Austen and Ourselves

READING THE SIX NOVELS, again and again, is not enough. Fans of Jane Austen seem to be particularly active in their devotion. Jane Austen is everywhere today.

The Jane Austen industry

Ranging from rigorous scholarship through to downright commercialism, and encountering a lot of amateur enthusiasm on the way, the Jane Austen industry is a source of enjoyment and a boost to the economy at the same time.

At one end of the spectrum Jane Austen is claimed as their own by the academics. She is well established on university syllabuses and the national curriculum for British state schools, as well as schools all over world, whether English is a first or foreign language.

At the other end of the spectrum is the fun merchandise – usually emanating from the USA – which enables devotees to proclaim their allegiance: "I'd rather be reading Jane Austen" car stickers, "Born to be an heroine" T-shirts, "I think it was Jane Austen who said …" Post-its. Tote-bags, key-fobs and paperweights can all be purchased carrying an image of Jane Austen.

In Memory of
JANE AUSTEN,
youngeſt daughter of the late
Rev.d GEORGE AUSTEN,
formerly Rector of Steventon in this County
ſhe departed this Life on the 18th of July 1817,
aged 41, after a long illneſs ſupported with
the patience and the hopes of a Chriſtian.
The benevolence of her heart,
the ſweetneſs of her temper, and
the extraordinary endowments of her mind
obtained the regard of all who knew her, and
the warmeſt love of her intimate connections.
Their grief is in proportion to their affection
they know their loſs to be irreparable,
but in their deepeſt affliction they are conſoled
by a firm though humble hope that her charity,
devotion, faith and purity, have rendered
her ſoul acceptable in the ſight of her
REDEEMER.

JANE AUSTEN'S MEMORIAL STONE IN WINCHESTER CATHEDRAL.

Between these extremes are the books and articles published for the academic and general reader in increasing numbers: 27 books and 22 articles in both learned journals and newspapers during 1995 alone. There are audio cassettes, both abridged and unabridged, and video recordings of TV and film adaptations. Several actresses specialize in touring one-woman performances impersonating Jane Austen.

Tour operators, study holiday organizations and departments for continuing education regularly offer Jane Austen weeks or weekends, in which lectures and discussion of the novels is balanced by visits to places associated with the novelist. Many people make their own private pilgrimages, tramping the streets of Bath, Lyme Regis, and London in quest of the buildings she knew, knocking on the door of the house in Winchester where she died, or getting lost in the lanes of North Hampshire looking for the field in which Steventon Rectory once stood.

The Jane Austen Society

The Jane Austen Society in the United Kingdom was founded in the 1940s when the purchase and preservation of Chawton Cottage was at issue. This burden was removed by the timely benefaction of Mr Carpenter. The Jane Austen Memorial Trust set up to administer the museum remains quite separate from the Society, which continues to thrive as an organization whose objective is to promote enjoyment and understanding of the life and work of Jane Austen. Present membership stands at over 2,000.

The Society became fully democratic in 1994 with the election by ballot of its officers and committee, and it became a Registered Charity at the same date. Each year since 1949 it has published an *Annual Report* of its activities during the year, which is also a forum for Jane Austen research and a repository for information about new publications and the results of auctions of Jane Austen manuscripts and early editions.

Also printed in the Report is the Address given by the guest speaker at the AGM, held each year on the Saturday nearest to the anniversary of Jane Austen's death (18 July). Held in a marquee in the grounds of Chawton Manor, by kind permission of the owners, the AGM is usually attended by about 600 members and guests who make the journey from all parts of the country and from abroad to honour Jane Austen in the peaceful village that was her home.

Many distinguished speakers have accepted the invitation to address the Society, including, over the years, Harold Nicolson, Elizabeth Bowen, Elizabeth Jenkins and Margaret Drabble. Past Presidents of the Society have been the Duke of Wellington, Lord David Cecil and the Countess of Huntingdon. The current President is Richard Knight, descendant of Jane's brother Edward.

From the late 1980s, beginning in Bristol and Bath, regional branches of the Society began to be established by enthusiastic local members to organize events and meetings and promote any Jane Austen associations within their area. In Bath the branch has raised money for the preservation of the George Austen's gravestone in Walcot church, while in Kent a kneeler embroidered with the Austen arms has been sponsored and placed in Tonbridge church.

Jane Austen abroad

Meanwhile, in the bicentennial year of 1975, two enthusiasts on the North American continent, Joan Austen-Leigh from Vancouver and Jack David Grey from New York, decided to found a Jane Austen Society of North America, known affectionately as JASNA. Virtually every state of the USA and every province of Canada now has its own Chapter. On December 16 every year JASNA publishes its journal *Persuasions*, in which contributions from academic and non-academic members, both serious and entertaining, make for a stimulating read. Each October a four-day conference, attracting several hundred delagates who choose from a wealth of seminars and lectures on a previously chosen theme, takes place in a different part of the continent, from Lake Louise to New Orleans, from Richmond to Santa Monica. More recently the Jane Austen Society of Australia has been founded, with its own journal *Sensibilities*. So much activity all over the world – and all because one woman wrote six novels two hundred years ago.

THE HOUSE IN WINCHESTER WHERE JANE AUSTEN DIED.

Index

All numbers in *italics* refer to illustrations

Credits

Photographic Acknowledgements

The publisher would like to thank the following for their permission to reproduce photographs and illustrations in this book:

A descendant of Charles Austen 75; **AKG London** 77, 89, 90; **Alwyn Austen** 10 (Angelo Hornak) 47(b); **Joan Austen-Leigh** 137; **Aquarius** 134; **BBC** 13(t), 17, 49, 57, 120, 121(t & b), 123(b), 124, 129(t); **Bath Central Library** 34, 35, 45, 53; **Bridgeman Art Library** 1, 19, 28, 40, 54, 80, 83, 86, (Asprey & Co, London) 61, (British Library) 79, 115(br), (Chawton House, Hants) 36, 48, (Christies) 38, 47(t), 66, (City of Bristol Museum & Art Gallery) 7, 55, 68, (Crescent Art Gallery, Scarborough) 110, (Fitzwilliam Museum, Cambridge) 100, (Heeresgeschichtliches Museum, Vienna) 59, (John Noott Galleries, Broadway, Worcs) 101, (Michael Gillingham Colln) 70, (Roy Miles Gallery, 29 Bruton St, London) 108, (Royal Albert Memorial Museum Exeter) 42, (Southampton City Art Gallery) 43, (Victoria & Albert Museum) 93(b), 99, 112; **British Library** 14, 31, 83(t), 129(b); **Christies Images** 103(t), 107(t); **John Crook, Winchester** 140(b); **English Heritage Photo Library** 106, 107(b), (The Iveagh Bequest, Kenwood) 94; **Mr and Mrs D Hopkinson** 136; **Images** 96; **Jane Austen Memorial Trust, Chawton** 18, 24, 26, 27, 44, 52, 58, 60, 131, 143, (Private Collection) 3, (Helen Lefroy) 13(b), (Jarrold Publishing) 53(b), 15, (Jarrold Publishing/Neil Jinkerson) 118, (Jane Austen Society) 16, (Mrs E Fowle) 22, 23, 71, (Mrs S Knight) 51(t & b), (photo Roy Fox) 29; **Knight Family Collection** 2, (Hampshire Record Office) 85(c); **J Lefroy, Carrigglas Manor, Co Longford** (A C Cooper) 30; **Mansell Collection** 32, 63(b), 67, 109, 111, 113, 115(tl); **Mary Evans Picture Library** 21, 46, 56, 62, 78, 82, 85(b), 87, 93(tr), 104, 114, 123(t), 125, 133, 144; **Meridian Broadcasting** 84(b), 116, 127; **Michael Edwards** 25; **Miramax** 126, 135(t); **National Gallery, London** 98; **National Library of Scotland** 39; **National Portrait Gallery, London** 12, 20, 91, 95; **National Trust Photo Library** 102, 105; **Peter Newarks Picture Library** (American Pictures) 81, (Historical Pictures) 64, 69, 74, 76(l), 76(c), 88, 92, (Military Pictures) 72, 73; **Pictorial Press** 135(b); **Rex Features** (Columbia Tristar Pictures) 119; **Southampton City Council** 37; **Sarah Larter** 138(b), 139, 143, 138(c); **Sheffield City Art Galleries** 33; **The Royal Collection copyright Her Majesty The Queen** 132; **Winchester Tourist Board** 130, 141

SPECIAL THANKS ARE DUE to Tom Carpenter of the Jane Austen Memorial Trust in Chawton, Hampshire, Alwyn Austen, Joan Austen-Leigh, Helen Lefroy, Joanna Hartley at Bridgeman Art Library, Nicola Horsey of Hampshire County Council, John Crook and Winchester Tourist Board for their particular help with locating or providing illustrations.

Every effort has been made to locate copyright holders or those whose permission is required to reproduce images and the publisher accepts their right to be credited in any future edition of this publication.

ENDPAPERS – Circular family tree showing Jane Austen's paternal and maternal ancestry (courtesy of Alwyn Austen).

INDEX by Colin Hynson

Jane Austen's House

CHAWTON COTTAGE

The museum is open 11 am–4.30 pm daily from March to December inclusive (except for Christmas and Boxing Day) and on Saturday and Sunday only in January and February.

Telephone: 01420 83262.

Jane Austen Hotline

For information about Jane Austen places and events in Hampshire:

telephone: 01703 629798
e-mail: http: //www.hants.gov.uk/austen

040-774-1

Jane Austen Societies

UNITED KINGDOM
The Jane Austen Society
Carton House
Redwood Lane
Medstead
Alton
Hampshire
GU34 5PE

AUSTRALIA & NEW ZEALAND
The Jane Austen Society of Australia
1 Queen's Road
Asquith
NSW 2077

CANADA & USA
The Jane Austen Society of North America

(Canada)
22 Kingsmount Boulevard
Sudbury
Ontario
P3E 1K9

(USA)
2650 D Matheson Way
Sacramento
CA 95864

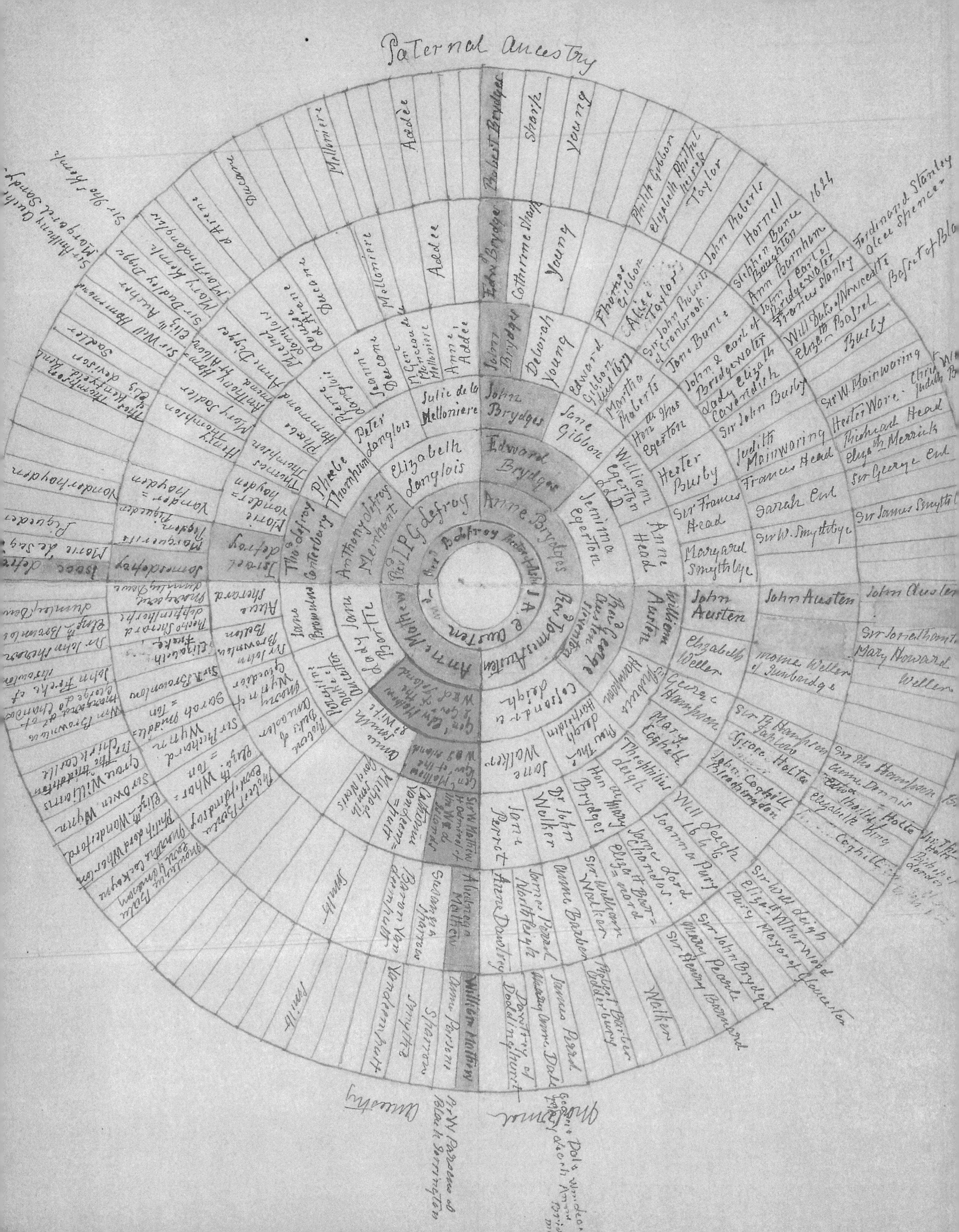

Paternal Ancestry
Anne Brydges
Edward Brydges
John Brydges
Deborah Young
Young
Addee
Catherine Sharp
Robert Brydges
Elizabeth Langlois
Peter Langlois
Julie de la Mellonière
Mellonière
Phoebe Thompson
Anthony defroy Merchant
Tho. defroy Canterbury
Jane Gibbon
Edward Gibbon
Thomas Gibbon
Martha Roberts
William Egerton LLD
Jemima Egerton
Anne Head
Hester Busby
Sir Frances Head
Margaret Smyth
Sarah Ent
Sir George Ent
Judith Mainwaring
Sir John Busby
Sir W. Mainwaring
Richard Head
John Austen
William Austen
Elizabeth Weller
Mary Howard
Weller
George Hampson
Mary Cogshill
Jane Walker
Dr John Walker
Theophilus Leigh
Cassandra Leigh
Will Leigh 1666
Sir Will Leigh
Sir John Brydges
Walker
Anne Barber
Anna Dowdry
Dorothy of Doddinghurst
Anne Perrot
Anne Matthew
William Matthew
Sir W. Parsons of Black Borrington
Ferdinand Stanley
1624